GCSE English Literature AQA Anthology

Unseen Poetry

Study and Practice Book

This book is a step-by-step guide to becoming an expert on
the Unseen Poetry part of your GCSE English Literature exam.

It's got everything you need — lots of poems,
worked examples, practice questions and exam advice.

It's ideal for use as a classroom study book
or a revision guide.

What CGP is all about

Our sole aim here at CGP is to produce the highest quality
books — carefully written, immaculately presented and
dangerously close to being funny.

Then we work our socks off to get them out to you
— at the cheapest possible prices.

CONTENTS

Section One — The Unseen Poetry Question

What You Have to do in the Exam 2
Five Steps to Analysing the Unseen Poem 3
Example Poetry Analysis 4

Section Two — About the Poets

\\\\ I I I I I I I I I I I I I I I I I I / /
If you're doing your exam in
2014, ignore Section 2. It's for
exams from June 2015 onwards.
/ I I I I I I I I I I I I I I I I I I I I \\\\

William Blake 7
John Keats 8
Christina Rossetti 9
Thomas Hardy 10
Robert Frost 11
Wilfred Owen 12
Dorothy Parker 13
W. H. Auden 14
Maya Angelou 15
Tony Harrison 16
Wendy Cope 17
Brian Patten 18
Jo Shapcott 19
Sophie Hannah 20
Owen Sheers 21

Section Three — Unseen Poetry Practice

Condolence — Dorothy Parker 22
Volumes — Jo Shapcott 24
Against Road-building — Sophie Hannah 26
The Sitter — Wendy Cope 28
The Dead-Beat — Wilfred Owen 30
The Tyger — William Blake 32
Jumper — Tony Harrison 34
History — Owen Sheers 36
On the Grasshopper and Cricket — John Keats 38
The More Loving One — W. H. Auden 40
Winter: My Secret — Christina Rossetti 42

CONTENTS

Section Four — Marking Exam Answers

Exam Advice 44
Mark Scheme 45
The Road Not Taken — Robert Frost 46
Sample Answers 47
Kin — Maya Angelou 48
Sample Answers 49
The Armada — Brian Patten 50
Sample Answers 51
'I Look Into My Glass' — Thomas Hardy 52
Sample Answers 53
Don't Say I Said — Sophie Hannah 54
Sample Answers 55

Section Five — Sample Exams

Long Distance II — Tony Harrison 56
The Send-Off — Wilfred Owen 57
Flowers — Wendy Cope 58
The Man He Killed — Thomas Hardy 59

Glossary 60
Acknowledgements 62

Published by CGP

Editors:
Claire Boulter, Rebecca Tate,
Jennifer Underwood.

Contributor:
Holly Bennett

With thanks to Heather Gregson and
Nicola Woodfin for the proofreading, and
Jan Greenway for the copyright research.

ISBN: 978 1 84762 325 6
Groovy website: www.cgpbooks.co.uk
Jolly bits of clipart from CorelDRAW®
Printed by Elanders Ltd, Newcastle upon Tyne.

Based on the classic CGP style created by Richard
Parsons.

What You Have to do in the Exam

As part of your GCSE AQA English Literature course, you'll have to do a poetry exam.
It's called Unit 2: Poetry Across Time. This page tells you what's involved.

The Exam has an Unseen Poetry Section

Your poetry exam has two sections. It will be split up like this:

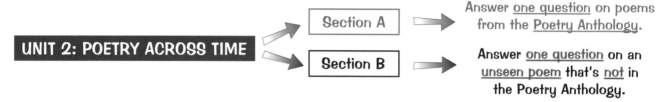

UNIT 2: POETRY ACROSS TIME

Section A → Answer one question on poems from the Poetry Anthology.

Section B → Answer one question on an unseen poem that's not in the Poetry Anthology.

This book shows you how to answer the unseen poetry question in Section B.

1) The whole exam lasts 1 hour 15 minutes.
2) Spend about 30 minutes on the unseen poetry question.
3) The question is worth 18 marks.

If you're taking your exam in 2014, you could be asked to analyse any poem. If you're taking it from 2015 onwards, the poem will be by one of fifteen poets who you'll have studied in class (see Section 2 for more).

You'll be Tested on Two Main Things

In your answer, you'll need to cover:

① What the poem is about — the poem's message, and its themes and ideas.

② How the poet communicates these ideas using language, structure and form.

Here's what you have to Do...

1) Read the question and underline the key words, i.e. what themes the question wants you to focus on, and what aspects of the poem's language and structure you have to look at.

2) Read the poem twice and analyse it using our five-point plan.
   Underline or make notes about the important bits.

   5 steps to analysing poetry

   1) Work out what the poem's about.
   2) Work out the purpose, theme or message.
   3) Explore the emotions, moods or feelings.
   4) Identify the poet's techniques.
   5) Think about your own feelings about the poem.

   See page 3 for more on this.

3) Plan your essay (spend about 5 minutes doing this) — pick out 3 or 4 good quotes, make sure you've got plenty to say about them, and include these in your plan.

4) Now you're ready to write your essay. Hurrah.

Five Steps to Analysing the Unseen Poem

When you've read through the unseen poem <u>twice</u>, there are <u>five main things</u> that you need to do.

1) Work out what the poem's About

Pick out the important bits of the poem as you read it — underline them or make notes.

1) Work out the <u>subject</u> of the poem.
   E.g. "The poem is about the narrator's relationship with his parents".
2) Look at whether it's written in the <u>first</u> person ("<u>I</u> felt"), <u>second</u> person ("<u>you</u> felt") or <u>third</u> person ("<u>he/she</u> felt"). Think about <u>who</u> the poem is <u>addressing</u> — e.g. the narrator's lover, the reader...

2) Identify the Purpose, Theme or Message

1) Think about <u>what</u> the poet is saying, <u>why</u> they've written the poem, or what <u>ideas</u> they're exploring.
2) The poem could be an <u>emotional response</u> to something. It might aim to <u>get a response</u> from the <u>reader</u>, or put across a message or an opinion about something.
3) There could be <u>more than one</u> purpose, theme or message in the poem.

3) Explore the Emotions, Moods or Feelings

1) Think about the <u>different emotions or feelings</u> in the poem.
2) Identify the poem's <u>mood</u> (the general <u>atmosphere</u>, e.g. gloomy).
3) Look at how the poet has used different <u>techniques</u> to show these emotions (see step 4).

4) Identify the Techniques used in the poem

1) Pick out the <u>different techniques</u> the poet has used and how they create the <u>emotions</u>, <u>moods</u> or <u>feelings</u> in the poem. These are all techniques that you've studied for the <u>Poetry Anthology</u>:

   - <u>Form</u> — things like <u>rhyme</u> and <u>rhythm</u>. You might recognise a particular <u>form</u>, e.g. a sonnet. Also look at <u>changes</u> in the lengths of <u>lines</u> or <u>stanzas</u>.
   - <u>Structure</u> — the <u>order of ideas</u> in the poem, as well as any <u>changes</u> in mood or <u>tone</u>.
   - <u>Poetic devices</u> — things like <u>alliteration</u>, <u>personification</u> and <u>enjambment</u>.
   - <u>Imagery</u> — language that creates a <u>picture in your mind</u>, including things like <u>metaphors</u> and <u>similes</u>.

   Have a look at the glossary on p.60-61 if you're not sure what these terms mean.

2) Think about <u>why</u> the poet has used these techniques, and what <u>effect</u> they create. Link the way the <u>techniques</u> work on the reader to the <u>ideas</u> the poet is exploring.

5) Include Your Thoughts and Feelings about the poem

1) Examiners love to hear what <u>you think</u> of a poem and how it makes <u>you feel</u>.
2) Think about how well the poem gets its <u>message</u> across and what <u>impact</u> it had on you.
3) Try <u>not</u> to use "<u>I</u>" though — don't say "I felt sad that the narrator's brother died", it's much <u>better</u> to say "It makes <u>the reader</u> feel the narrator's sense of sadness at the death of his brother."
4) Think about any <u>other ways</u> that the poem could be <u>interpreted</u>.

The purpose of poems — keeping poets in employment...

Phew — there's a lot to take in here. Luckily the next few pages take you through a lovely <u>worked example</u>, so when you come to analyse an unseen poem yourself, it'll be <u>easy as pie</u>. A nice apple one.

Example Poetry Analysis

Read the question, then annotate the poem to pick out the important bits. Here's an example...

Here's a Sample exam question...

Read 'His Visitor'. What is the poet saying about death and the afterlife? How does he present these ideas?

What's the poem's message about death and what happens after death?

What techniques does the poet use to get his message across?

This is how you might Annotate the Poem...

Read through the poem, and mark any bits of it that stand out.
Jot down your thoughts too — it'll help you plan your essay (see p.5).

Annotate your poem in any way that works for you — underline, highlight or scribble notes.

His Visitor

Subject — a woman revisits her old house.

Voice — first person narrator.

I come across from Mellstock* while the moon wastes weaker
To behold where I lived with you for twenty years and more:
I shall go in the grey, at the passing of the mail-train,
And need no setting open of the long familiar door
 As before

Door doesn't need opening — speaker is ghost.

5

The change I notice in my once own quarters!
A formal-fashioned border where the daisies used to be,
The rooms new painted, and the pictures altered,
And other cups and saucers, and no cosy nook for tea
 As with me.

Changes in physical setting and people.

10

I discern the dim faces of the sleep-wrapt servants;
They are not those who tended me through feeble hours and strong,
But strangers quite, who never knew my rule here,
Who never saw me painting, never heard my softling song
 Float along.

Sight is 'dim' — barrier between living and dead.

15

So I don't want to linger in this re-decked dwelling,
I feel too uneasy at the contrasts I behold,
And I make again for Mellstock to return here never,
And rejoin the roomy silence, and the mute and manifold
 Souls of old.

We sympathise with speaker's sense of loss.

Long lines and gentle, regular rhythm give sad tone.

20

Thomas Hardy (1840 - 1928)

Mood — dark night, creepy.

Rhyme scheme: ABCBB. Final line 3 syllables — slows pace and gives ghostly feel.

Exclamation mark shows disbelief.

Repetition of 'and' emphasises changes and makes speaker sound angry.

Another woman?

Alliteration — contrasts with "mute" dead.

Mood — ghostly voice.

Links with line one — speaker returning to graveyard

Surrounded by silent ghosts.

Mellstock — Hardy's name for the place where his first wife was buried.
mail-train — a train that carried mail during the night.
discern — make out.
softling — soft and delicate.
manifold — many and varied.

Example Poetry Analysis

So, you've <u>read</u> the poem and have some <u>ideas</u> about how you might answer the <u>question</u>. The next step is to turn your scribblings into a detailed <u>essay plan</u>. This page tells you exactly how to do it — some would say that's coincidence, I call it fate.

Make an <u>Essay Plan</u> <u>before you start</u>

1) You've only got about <u>5 minutes</u> to plan, so keep it <u>short</u>.
2) Focus on <u>three or four key quotes</u> from the poem.
3) Don't forget to write about <u>what</u> the poet says and <u>how</u> they say it.

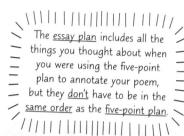

The <u>essay plan</u> includes all the things you thought about when you were using the five-point plan to annotate your poem, but they <u>don't</u> have to be in the <u>same order</u> as the <u>five-point plan</u>.

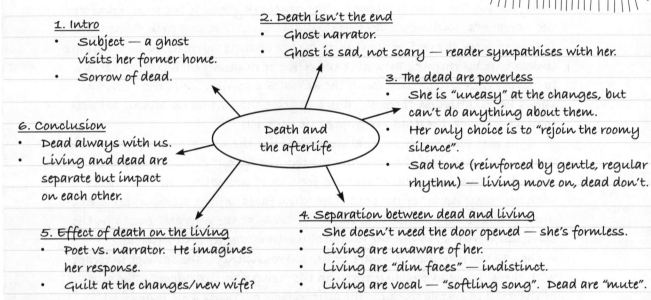

<u>1. Intro</u>
• Subject — a ghost visits her former home.
• Sorrow of dead.

<u>2. Death isn't the end</u>
• Ghost narrator.
• Ghost is sad, not scary — reader sympathises with her.

<u>3. The dead are powerless</u>
• She is "uneasy" at the changes, but can't do anything about them.
• Her only choice is to "rejoin the roomy silence".
• Sad tone (reinforced by gentle, regular rhythm) — living move on, dead don't.

Death and the afterlife

<u>6. Conclusion</u>
• Dead always with us.
• Living and dead are separate but impact on each other.

<u>5. Effect of death on the living</u>
• Poet vs. narrator. He imagines her response.
• Guilt at the changes/new wife?

<u>4. Separation between dead and living</u>
• She doesn't need the door opened — she's formless.
• Living are unaware of her.
• Living are "dim faces" — indistinct.
• Living are vocal — "softling song". Dead are "mute".

4) Now you've got a <u>plan</u> for your essay, you just need to <u>write</u> the thing, but today's your lucky day, because I've done this one for you...

Here's a <u>Model Answer...</u>

Use your essay plan to make sure you keep to the point.

Clear start, showing that you've understood the poem.

Good use of quotes to back up points.

    The poem 'His Visitor' describes the return of a ghost to the home she shared with her partner for "twenty years and more". In it, the poet imagines her resentment of the changes that have occurred since her death, indirectly revealing his own guilt at allowing these changes to take place. The poem suggests that although the living can affect the dead, and vice versa, ultimately they are separate states with no point of contact.
    The most obvious point the poet makes about death is that it is not the end. Although the narrator of the poem never explicitly states that she is a ghost, it is made clear when she says, for instance, that she arrives by night and needs "no setting open" of the door. The use of the first person makes the reader empathise with the sadness of the narrator, breaking down the stereotype of ghosts being frightening.

Write about the poem's main messages early on in your essay.

Give a personal response to the poem.

Example Poetry Analysis

Whew, nearly at the end of the first section — read the rest of the <u>model answer</u>, then you've just got time for a cuppa and a biscuit before you move on to <u>Section Two</u>.

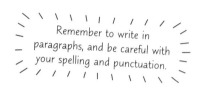
Remember to write in paragraphs, and be careful with your spelling and punctuation.

Write about feelings and mood, and use quotes to back up your points.

The feeling of sorrow is emphasised by the powerlessness of the narrator. Although she is "uneasy" at the changes that have been made to her former home, the only way she can ease her discomfort is to leave and "return here never". Death therefore involves giving up a loved home and all that is familiar, and instead accepting the loneliness that comes with joining the "roomy silence". The gentle rhythm of the poem reinforces the narrator's loneliness. The three syllable lines that end each stanza are separated from the rest of the stanza by the change in rhythm, but they are linked to it by rhyme. They have the effect of making each stanza seem to tail off wistfully, reinforcing the narrator's sorrow, while their content shows her fixation on "before". This suggests that, while the living are able to move forward, the dead are trapped in the past.

Comment on form and the effect it has.

The poet also suggests that death divides the narrator from the living world. The colours of the poem are muted: the "grey" of night and the moon that "wastes weaker" create a feeling of unreality that contrasts with the "cosy nook" of the past. The "dim faces" of the sleeping servants may be shadowy because it is night, or because the narrator exists in the spiritual world, so to her, the material world is vague and unclear. Although the narrator is aware of her surroundings, she cannot interact with them, instead passing through the "long familiar door". The silence of the dead is emphasised by the alliteration of "mute and manifold", which contrasts with the "softling song" of the narrator when she was alive.

Write about any imagery in the poem.

Think about different interpretations to help you get top marks.

Mention and explain any poetic devices that you spot.

Think about any hidden meanings the poem might contain.

The poem also gives clues about the impact of death on the living. By imagining how "uneasy" the narrator feels at the "contrasts" she sees, Hardy gives the reader a hint of the guilt he feels at moving on while she cannot. The changes described are not large, but the use of an exclamation mark and the repetition of "and" in the second stanza shows how significant the poet believes they would have been to the narrator. The mention of "other cups and saucers", traditionally chosen by women, hint that the dead woman's place may have been taken by another woman. This may explain the poet's guilt. However, the fact that he is so concerned with what the ghost would feel suggests, ironically, that he has not really moved on.

Mention specific language features and explain why the poet used them.

Give a good personal response wherever you can.

The central message of the poem is that the living and the dead inhabit two separate worlds. Hardy explores this through his use of a ghostly first-person narrator, a gentle regular rhythm which reflects her sad drifting around the house and her eventual return to "roomy silence".

Sum up the <u>what</u> and <u>how</u> in your final paragraph.

Mute and Manifold Dead — out now on DVD...

I rented it last week. It wasn't great — if you've seen someone miming how upset they are about the new teacups once, you've seen it a thousand times. Still, if that's your sort of thing, go ahead.

William Blake

If you're doing your exam in 2014, ignore this section. It's for exams from June 2015 onwards.

In your Unit 2 exam you'll have to <u>analyse</u> a poem by one of <u>15 set poets</u>, so it's worth knowing a bit about them. Luckily this section gives you all the <u>info</u> you need. First up, <u>William Blake</u> (1757-1827).

Blake was <u>Ahead</u> of his <u>Time</u>

© Mary Evans Picture Library

1) William Blake was born in <u>London</u>. His mother taught him to read and write, and at the age of 14 he was <u>apprenticed</u> to an <u>engraver</u>.

2) Blake had some fairly <u>unusual views</u> for the time — he believed in <u>racial</u> and <u>sexual</u> <u>equality</u>, and he was <u>sympathetic</u> towards the French Revolutionaries and their aims (which included trying to overthrow the ruling classes). He also <u>disagreed</u> with many of the teachings of the <u>Church</u>.

3) He opened his own <u>print shop</u> in 1784, and printed <u>revolutionary political works</u>, as well as his own <u>poetry</u>.

4) Blake taught his <u>wife</u> to read and write, and she helped him to <u>print</u> and <u>illustrate</u> his work. His best-known poems were published in two volumes, '<u>Songs of Innocence</u>' and '<u>Songs of Experience</u>'.

Blake wrote about <u>Opposites</u>, <u>Innocence</u> and <u>Freedom</u>

1) **Opposites** — Blake was interested in the <u>tension</u> between different <u>forces</u> and <u>ways of being</u>, e.g. good and evil, reason and imagination, cruelty and kindness. Blake believed that all <u>opposites</u> had to exist together, and that it was <u>impossible</u> to understand one <u>without the other</u>.

2) **Innocence and Experience** — These are the <u>opposites</u> which feature most often in Blake's poetry. He saw innocence as a <u>child-like</u> state of <u>joy</u>, <u>imagination</u> and <u>intuition</u>, and experience as an <u>adult</u> state of <u>misery</u>, <u>reason</u> and <u>sin</u>. He writes about the <u>positives</u> and <u>negatives</u> of both states.

3) **Freedom** — Blake believed in <u>freedom</u> and <u>fighting oppression</u>. At the time, the <u>Church</u> and <u>upper classes</u> controlled the lives of ordinary people. Several of Blake's poems feature a character who <u>fights</u> against a <u>greater force</u> (<u>symbolising</u> these ruling groups).

Well-known poems	
• A Poison Tree	• The Lamb
• London	• The Tyger

Blake's 'Songs' are full of <u>Symbolism</u>, <u>Rhyme</u> and <u>Repetition</u>

1) **Symbolism** — Blake uses <u>natural objects</u> such as <u>plants</u> and <u>animals</u> to symbolise human <u>strengths</u> and <u>flaws</u>, as well as <u>institutions</u> like the Church. His symbols are sometimes described in a <u>child-like way</u>, e.g. the "woolly" lamb in 'The Lamb', which reinforces the fact that they are <u>symbolic</u> rather than real.

2) **Rhyme** — Most of Blake's poems have a <u>strong rhyme scheme</u> and a <u>regular rhythm</u>. Many of them have a <u>sing-song</u> quality, like a nursery rhyme. This makes them seem <u>simple</u>, but they have <u>hidden</u> meanings.

3) **Repetition** — Blake often <u>repeats</u> a particular <u>word</u>, <u>sentence</u> or <u>idea</u>. This emphasises the <u>point</u> he is making, but also adds to the <u>nursery rhyme</u> feel of his poems.

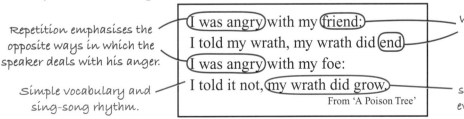

Repetition emphasises the opposite ways in which the speaker deals with his anger.

Simple vocabulary and sing-song rhythm.

I was angry with my friend; I told my wrath, my wrath did end I was angry with my foe: I told it not, my wrath did grow.

From 'A Poison Tree'

Whole poem written in rhyming couplets.

The speaker's anger is symbolised by a tree, which eventually kills his enemy.

Blake kept repeating himself — bet that was annoying...

William Blake was unusual — he wasn't particularly well-educated or rich like the other poets of his day. He was very critical of the Church, inequality in society and politics, and he wasn't afraid to say it.

John Keats

John Keats (1795-1821) trained as a surgeon before deciding he wanted to be a poet. Unfortunately his career as a poet didn't last long, as he died young. He still managed to write a lot of famous poems though...

Keats Died Young

© iStockphoto.com/Wynter

1) John Keats was affected by death at a young age. His father died in an accident when Keats was eight and his mother died of tuberculosis when he was 14.

2) He never married, but he was secretly engaged to a woman called Fanny Brawne when he died.

3) Keats caught tuberculosis and died in 1821 in Rome — he was only 25.

4) Keats's poems weren't very famous when he was alive, and he got some pretty bad reviews for some of them. He only really became famous after he'd died.

He often wrote about Death, Change, Nature and Love

1) **Death** — Keats wrote a lot about death and its inevitability. This might have been a result of the early deaths of his parents and brother.

2) **Change** — Keats wrote about the contrasts between temporary and permanent things. He believed that the most beautiful things were alive and therefore temporary — they could only be preserved forever through art. By writing poems about beautiful things he hoped to preserve them.

3) **Nature** — Keats was often inspired by nature. Nature is used as a metaphor e.g. a calm sea symbolises peace.

4) **Love** — Some of Keats's poems are about the pain of loving someone you can't be with.

Well-known poems
- To Autumn
- Bright Star
- Ode to a Nightingale
- Ode on a Grecian Urn

Keats writes Traditional poems full of Symbolism

1) **Symbolism** — Some of Keats's symbols include the ancient world, which represents permanence even though life is short, nature, which represents different emotions, and music which represents poetry.

2) **Traditional Form** — A lot of Keats's poems take the form of traditional sonnets or odes. Sonnets have a very set regular rhyme scheme and a constant number of syllables per line. Odes don't have a consistent form, but they always praise someone or something. He often writes in iambic pentameter as well.

3) **Addressed to Inhuman Things** — Keats often addresses things that aren't human (e.g. animals, birds or a star) as if they were human and could reply to him.

Reference to ancient world shows that the nightingale's song lasts forever

Thou wast not born for death, immortal Bird!
No hungry generations tread thee down;
The voice I hear this passing night was heard
In ancient days by emperor and clown

From 'Ode to a Nightingale'

Addressed to the nightingale

Regular rhyme scheme

Iambic pentameter

Keats keeps a keen parakeet called Keith...

It can be hard to get past the language in Keats's poems. It's quite old-fashioned, but that's because he was writing quite a while ago. Stick with it, and look out for the symbols he uses.

Christina Rossetti

Christina Rossetti (1830-1894) is one of the best-known female poets of the <u>Victorian</u> era. Knowing a bit about her <u>life</u> will help you understand her <u>poems</u>. Luckily, this page tells you everything you need to know.

Rossetti came from a Family of Artists

1) Christina Rossetti was born into a very <u>artistic</u> family — her father was a <u>poet</u>, her uncle was a <u>writer</u> and her older brother was a <u>painter</u>.

2) She started <u>writing poetry</u> when she was <u>eleven</u>. Her <u>first book</u> of poems was <u>published</u> by her grandfather, who owned a printing press (handy).

3) Rossetti <u>fell ill</u> when she was in her <u>teens</u> and, although she lived well into her sixties, she never fully <u>recovered</u>.

4) She was <u>deeply religious</u>. She broke off several relationships because her suitors didn't share her strong <u>faith</u>.

© Mary Evans Picture Library

Her main Themes are Death, Love, Religion and Sin

1) `Death` — perhaps because of her long-term <u>illness</u>, lots of Rossetti's poems are about <u>death</u>. Several of them dwell on her <u>own death</u>, but she generally seems <u>fascinated</u> by it, rather than <u>frightened</u> of it.

2) `Love` — Rossetti wrote about <u>romantic love</u>, <u>religious love</u> and love of <u>family</u>. She <u>challenged</u> the common Victorian belief that marriage was the <u>central aim</u> of a woman's life — several of her strong female characters choose divine love (love of God) <u>above</u> romantic love.

3) `Religion` — some of Rossetti's poems are about <u>biblical events</u>, such as Christ's death and resurrection. She also wrote <u>hymns</u>, including the Christmas carol 'In the Bleak Midwinter'.

4) `Sin` — several of her poems feature women who <u>suffer</u> after having <u>sex outside of marriage</u> (a big no-no in Victorian times).

Well-known poems
- Remember
- A Birthday
- Goblin Market
- Sister Maude
- Song
- Cousin Kate

Her poems are Simple, Personal and use lots of Symbolism

1) `Simplicity` — many of her poems have a <u>strong rhyme scheme</u>, <u>short lines</u> and <u>simple vocabulary</u>, which means that they're quite <u>easy</u> to read and understand (though there are often <u>hidden meanings</u>).

2) `First person viewpoint` — lots of Rossetti's poems are written from the <u>point of view</u> of the <u>narrator</u> and use words like '<u>I</u>' and '<u>me</u>'. This makes them seem <u>personal</u>.

3) `Symbolism` — for example, <u>eating fruit</u> often symbolises <u>sin</u> and the <u>loss of innocence</u>, <u>plants</u> or <u>flowers</u> symbolise <u>life</u>, and <u>seasons</u> represent the journey from life to <u>death</u>.

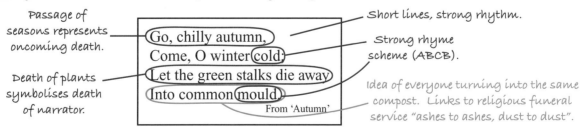

Passage of seasons represents oncoming death.

Short lines, strong rhythm.

Go, chilly autumn,
Come, O winter cold;
Let the green stalks die away
Into common mould.
From 'Autumn'

Strong rhyme scheme (ABCB).

Death of plants symbolises death of narrator.

Idea of everyone turning into the same compost. Links to religious funeral service "ashes to ashes, dust to dust".

This page symbolises my triumph over adversity...

If you want to get to grips with Rossetti, have a look on the internet for her poem 'Next of Kin'. Pick out all the metaphors for life and death, then write some notes explaining how she feels about death.

Thomas Hardy

Thomas Hardy (1840-1928) was a <u>prolific</u> chap — he wrote nearly a <u>thousand</u> poems in his lifetime. So you go and read those, and I'll see you back here in a few weeks. Oh go on then, read the <u>page</u> instead.

Hardy wrote some *Controversial Novels*

© Mary Evans Picture Library

1) Thomas Hardy was <u>born</u> and <u>raised</u> in a village in <u>Dorset</u>. His family wasn't very <u>rich</u> — his father was a stonemason and his mother was a cook.

2) At sixteen he became an apprentice <u>architect</u>, a job that he did for <u>many years</u>.

3) Hardy wrote <u>more than ten novels</u>, including 'Tess of the d'Urbervilles' and 'Jude the Obscure'. His novels were often <u>controversial</u> — they included <u>sex</u> and <u>unhappy marriages</u>. Hardy was <u>upset</u> by what people said about them, and decided to write <u>poetry</u> instead.

4) He <u>married twice</u>. Despite <u>drifting apart</u> from his <u>first</u> wife, Emma, Hardy was deeply <u>shocked</u> by her death and some of his most <u>famous poems</u> are about her.

His poems cover *Lots* of *Themes*

Hardy wrote <u>loads</u> of poems, so it's not surprising that they cover lots of different <u>themes</u>. Some of the <u>more common</u> ones are:

Well-known poems
- **The Voice**
- **The Ruined Maid**
- **The Darkling Thrush**
- **After a Journey**

1) `Nature` — Hardy's <u>childhood</u> in <u>rural Dorset</u> had a big effect on his poetry. He writes a lot about <u>plants</u>, <u>animals</u>, <u>landscapes</u> and <u>rural life</u>.

2) `Time` — A lot of Hardy's poems are about the <u>passage of time</u>. He sees time as an <u>unfriendly force</u> that brings <u>change</u> (usually for the <u>worse</u>), such as physical <u>ageing</u>, <u>death</u> and <u>loss of love</u>.

3) `Disappointment and grief` — Many of Hardy's poems are <u>sad</u>. They focus on <u>disappointment</u> in <u>love</u> and <u>life</u>, and <u>grief</u> for people who have <u>died</u> (especially his first wife).

Hardy uses a *Range* of *Poetic Techniques*

1) `Form` — Hardy experimented with different <u>forms</u>, <u>line lengths</u> and <u>rhyme schemes</u>. Most of his poems <u>rhyme</u> — he was interested in the way that rhyme affected the <u>rhythm</u> and <u>pace</u> of a poem.

2) `Unusual words` — Hardy often made <u>new words</u> by adding a <u>prefix</u> or combining two <u>existing words</u>. Some of his poems feature Dorset <u>dialect words</u> (e.g. "spudding" to mean digging), and <u>old words</u> that have fallen out of use (e.g. "ere" to mean before). This gives his poems a distinctive <u>voice</u>.

3) `Techniques` — A lot of Hardy's poems use <u>personification</u> and <u>alliteration</u>. He uses lots of <u>symbols</u> (especially <u>natural</u> symbols like plants, birds and seasons) to represent <u>life</u>, <u>death</u> and the <u>passage of time</u>.

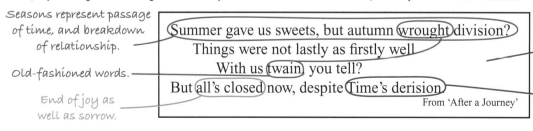

Seasons represent passage of time, and breakdown of relationship.

Old-fashioned words.

End of joy as well as sorrow.

Summer gave us sweets, but autumn wrought division?
Things were not lastly as firstly well
With us twain, you tell?
But all's closed now, despite Time's derision
From 'After a Journey'

Varying line lengths gives irregular rhythm and varies pace.

Personification of time as cruel and teasing.

I'd get in trouble for origiventing words...

There's a lot to get to grips with when you read Hardy's poems. If you want some practice, read 'The Darkling Thrush' (available online) and have a think about how Hardy talks about life and death.

Robert Frost

Robert Frost (1874-1963) lived in the USA for most of his life, and is considered to be one of America's greatest poets. It's kind of interesting, then, that his first book of poems was originally published in the UK.

Frost was a Famous American Poet

© REX/SNAP

1) Frost had an unhappy life. He lost his father when he was quite young, and several of his children died before he did.

2) His first poem was published in a magazine when Frost was quite young, but it was another 20 years before his first book of poetry was published.

3) In the meantime, he spent time working as a teacher and running a farm. He lived in the UK for almost three years, but spent most of his life living in the USA.

4) Frost read his poem 'The Gift Outright' at the inauguration of US President John F. Kennedy in 1961. He was the first poet to have this honour.

His Themes include Nature, Ageing and Everyday Life

1) **Nature** — Frost believed that nature could have a huge effect on people. His poems often talk about different characters' experiences of nature.

2) **Ageing** — In a career that spanned decades, it's not surprising that Frost wrote about ageing, and about the loss of youth. He writes about young people taking their freedom and innocence for granted.

3) **Everyday Life** — Frost's poems focus on normal people having normal experiences. He found deeper meanings in these everyday experiences. Frost talks about everyday life in a realistic way, which made his poems very accessible to everyone at the time he was writing.

Well-known poems
- The Road Not Taken
- Stopping by Woods on a Snowy Evening
- Bereft
- The Gift Outright

He uses Simple Language and Description

1) **Simple Language** — Using simple language helps Frost explore complex emotions and themes such as loss and death in a way that people can understand.

2) **Description** — Many of Frost's poems contain detailed descriptions of scenes, people or conversations. These descriptions give the reader a real sense of the settings of his poems, and the characters in them.

3) **Techniques** — Some of Frost's poems have a strong rhyme scheme, whereas others are written in blank verse to mimic the sound of natural speech. Frost often uses techniques like alliteration and assonance. All these things mean that his poems work best when they're read aloud.

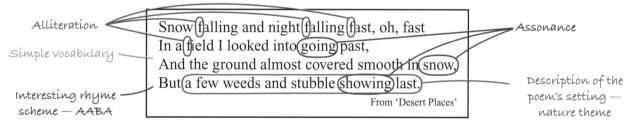

Alliteration
Simple vocabulary
Interesting rhyme scheme — AABA

Snow falling and night falling fast, oh, fast
In a field I looked into going past,
And the ground almost covered smooth in snow,
But a few weeds and stubble showing last.
From 'Desert Places'

Assonance
Description of the poem's setting — nature theme

A poem about a snowy evening — sounds Frost-y...

So Frost writes about places a lot — mostly ones that he sees on his way to somewhere else. Makes me wonder whether he was late for everything because he kept having to stop and write a poem...

Wilfred Owen

Wilfred Owen (1893-1918) is one of the <u>most famous</u> poets who wrote during the <u>First World War</u>. Most of his poems were written in a <u>very short period</u> (only a couple of years) during <u>World War I</u>.

Owen fought in the First World War

1) Wilfred Owen was born in <u>Shropshire</u> in <u>1893</u>.

2) The <u>First World War</u> began in <u>1914</u>. Owen joined the <u>army</u> the next year and ended up going to fight in northern France.

3) In 1917 he had a <u>breakdown</u>, suffering from '<u>shell-shock</u>'. He was sent to a military hospital where he met Siegfried Sassoon, a poet who <u>influenced</u> Owen's work.

World War I lasted from 1914 to 1918. In total, around 9 million men died, and tens of millions of others were injured.

4) He returned to France in 1918, and was <u>killed</u> on the 4th November 1918 — a <u>week</u> before the war <u>ended</u>.

5) Most of his poems were published <u>after</u> he <u>died</u>. They focused on <u>life</u> in the <u>trenches</u> and were very <u>successful</u>.

His main Themes are the Reality of War and Injury

1) **Reality of War** — Many people in Britain saw war as <u>glorious</u> and <u>noble</u>, and many <u>other war poets</u> wrote <u>patriotic</u> poems to <u>support</u> these views and <u>encourage</u> men to fight. Owen <u>attacked</u> this <u>propaganda</u> by writing about what war was <u>really like</u> for the men in the <u>trenches</u> — painful, disgusting and terrifying. Owen referred to the <u>waste of human life</u> and the <u>pointlessness</u> of combat as the '<u>Pity of War</u>'.

2) **Injury** — Many of Owen's poems show the terrible <u>effects of the war</u> on the soldiers fighting it. These might be <u>physical</u> or <u>mental</u> injuries. Owen often uses damage to <u>physical landscapes</u> (e.g. shell craters) to symbolise damage to the <u>human body</u>.

> **Well-known poems**
> * Anthem for Doomed Youth
> * Dulce et Decorum Est
> * Futility

Owen uses Narrative and Vivid Imagery

1) **Narrative** — He usually <u>tells a story</u> in his poems, often about an individual soldier. This helps the reader <u>connect</u> with the poem as it's easier to think about <u>one soldier</u> than <u>thousands</u>.

2) **Imagery** — People at home had <u>no idea</u> what war was <u>really</u> like, so Owen used vivid, realistic and horrifying <u>images</u> of <u>injury</u>, <u>suffering</u> and <u>death</u> to make them understand the <u>reality</u> of war.

3) **Sound Patterns** — Owen often uses <u>strong rhyme schemes</u>, <u>alliteration</u>, <u>onomatopoeia</u> and <u>assonance</u>. These techniques make his poems <u>forceful</u> and emphasise the <u>horror</u> of what he's describing.

4) **Direct speech** — Owen's poems often contain bits of <u>direct speech</u>. This helps the reader <u>feel</u> as if they're actually <u>there</u>. It also gives a <u>voice</u> to <u>individual soldiers</u> who may have died.

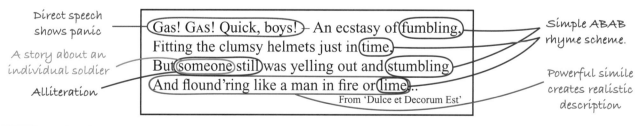

Direct speech shows panic

A story about an individual soldier

Alliteration

> Gas! GAS! Quick, boys! — An ecstasy of fumbling,
> Fitting the clumsy helmets just in time.
> But someone still was yelling out and stumbling
> And flound'ring like a man in fire or lime...
> From 'Dulce et Decorum Est'

Simple ABAB rhyme scheme.

Powerful simile creates realistic description

I'm too depressed to write anything funny here...

Owen did write some poems before the war, but to be honest they're a bit... well, dull. It's only when he writes about his terrible experiences of war that you can really feel his emotions in his poems.

Dorothy Parker

Dorothy Parker (1893-1967) wrote lots of <u>poems</u>, <u>short stories</u> and <u>reviews</u> from the 1910s to the 1960s. It helps that most of her poems are really short, but she still achieved a <u>massive amount</u> in her career.

Parker was *Funny but Unhappy*

1) Dorothy Parker grew up in New York and had a <u>difficult childhood</u>.
2) She wrote for <u>fashion magazines</u> and newspapers, was a successful screenwriter, and published lots of poetry and short stories. She was a rich <u>socialite</u> (she loved a <u>party</u>), and was well-known on the New York <u>literary scene</u> as well.
3) She had <u>difficult relationships</u> — she married <u>three times</u>, twice to the same man. She was often <u>unhappy</u>, and even attempted <u>suicide</u>.
4) She was interested in <u>politics</u>, believed strongly in <u>equality</u>, and left her money to <u>Martin Luther King</u>, a leader in the <u>black civil rights movement</u>.

She often wrote about *Relationships, Society and Death*

1) **Relationships** — Many of Parker's poems are about <u>relationships</u>, often <u>unequal</u> ones, and <u>break-ups</u>. She can be quite <u>harsh</u> about men.
2) **Society** — Parker uses poetry to <u>criticise</u> the <u>double standards</u> in how men and women were expected to behave (e.g. men could <u>sleep around</u> without being criticised), and the <u>different roles</u> of <u>women</u> in society.
3) **Death** — A lot of Parker's poems are about <u>death</u>. She writes about her <u>own death</u>, the death of others, <u>suicide</u> and <u>grief</u>. She often uses <u>dark humour</u> to express her interest in this theme.

Well-known poems
- I Know I Have Been Happiest
- Interior
- Men
- "Star Light, Star Bright—"
- A Well-Worn Story

Her poems are often *Short, Funny and Simple*

1) **Short poems** — Lots of Parker's poems are <u>very short</u>, and they usually just put across <u>one idea</u> or <u>emotion</u>. This means that they have a <u>big impact</u> on the reader.
2) **Humour** — There is dark <u>humour</u> and <u>sarcasm</u> in Parker's poems, and she uses <u>satire</u> even when she's writing about a <u>traumatic</u> subject. She often starts out quite <u>upbeat</u>, using <u>conventional</u> <u>imagery</u>, but then adds in a <u>twist</u> at the end to change the meaning of the poem and get you <u>thinking</u>.
3) **Simplicity** — Parker's <u>vocabulary</u> and <u>rhyme schemes</u> are often quite <u>simple</u>. She also tends to write in the <u>first person</u> which makes her poems seem more <u>personal</u>. This reflects the <u>simple</u> and <u>familiar subject matter</u> of her poems e.g. relationships.

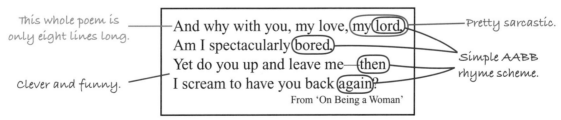

This whole poem is only eight lines long.

And why with you, my love, my lord,
Am I spectacularly bored,
Yet do you up and leave me then
I scream to have you back again?
From 'On Being a Woman'

Pretty sarcastic.
Simple AABB rhyme scheme.
Clever and funny.

"I don't care what is written about me so long as it isn't true..." (Dorothy Parker)
So Dorothy Parker's life was pretty depressing... It's a good thing her poetry's really hilarious, then. What? It's only funny in a really dark, depressing way? Oh dear, I'm going to need a sit down.

W. H. Auden

W. H. Auden (1907-1973) was a great poet, but he wasn't much good at titles. His first two books of poems were both called 'Poems' (confusing) and lots of his poems don't have titles at all (not very imaginative).

W. H. Auden wrote Hundreds of Poems

© REX/CSU Archives/Everett

1) Auden started writing poems when he was only 13, and published about 400 of them during his life, which is pretty good going.

2) His early poems copied the style of other poets, but he later developed his own style. He kept the ability to write many different styles of poem though.

3) He travelled a lot, going to Iceland, China, and many countries in Europe.

4) He grew up in the UK, but moved to the USA in 1939 and became a US citizen in 1946.

Auden's poetry covers Many Different Themes

Auden wrote about many different themes, but here are some of the more common ones:

1) `Politics` — Lots of Auden's poems talk about politics, and what was going on in the world at the time.

2) `Real Life` — Auden chose to write about real people, real places and real life.

3) `Moral Issues` — Auden wrote about right and wrong, and the moral choices that people make. For example, he questions the way that people act during war, and whether these actions are driven by evil.

4) `Love` — Auden wrote many love poems. They focused on the fragility of love, and were usually about particular relationships that he'd had, rather than love in general.

Well-known poems
• Funeral Blues
• Refugee Blues
• If I Could Tell You
• Night Mail

Auden's poems are Direct but full of Imagery

Auden's poems use a wide range of styles and forms. Here are some of his more common techniques:

1) `Imagery` — Auden often uses similes, metaphors and personification in his poems. This makes it easier for the reader to imagine the person or thing he is writing about.

2) `Conciseness` — His poems are often very direct, with no wasted words. Sometimes he even misses out short words like 'she', 'he' or 'the'. This gives his poems a sense of urgency and shifts the focus onto the more important words in the poem.

3) `Enjambment` — Many of Auden's poems use enjambment (when a sentence flows from one line to the next). This emphasises the words at the end of one line and at the beginning of the next.

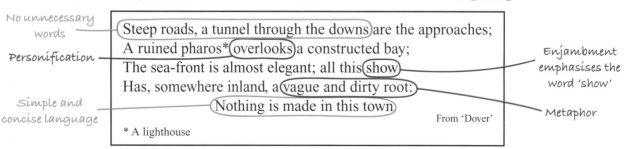

No unnecessary words

Personification

Simple and concise language

Steep roads, a tunnel through the downs are the approaches;
A ruined pharos* overlooks a constructed bay;
The sea-front is almost elegant; all this show
Has, somewhere inland, a vague and dirty root:
Nothing is made in this town

From 'Dover'
* A lighthouse

Enjambment emphasises the word 'show'

Metaphor

Auden — "Poetry makes nothing happen"...

... but it could help you pass your poetry exam... The meaning of Auden's poems isn't always obvious at first. Don't panic if you get one in the exam — just read it through a few times before you start.

Maya Angelou

Maya Angelou (1928-present) is a <u>poet</u>, <u>writer</u>, <u>actress</u> and <u>filmmaker</u>. She also used to be a <u>dancer</u>. And a <u>singer</u>. And a <u>journalist</u>. And a <u>civil rights activist</u>. Oh, and she knows at least <u>six languages</u>...

Maya Angelou has had a Difficult Life

1) Maya Angelou had a <u>difficult childhood</u> in the Southern USA. Her parents <u>divorced</u> when she was only three, and at the age of eight she was <u>abused</u> by her mother's boyfriend.

2) This time in her life was so <u>terrible</u> that she became <u>mute</u> — she didn't speak for almost five years. She began to speak again by <u>reading poetry aloud</u>.

3) She has experienced <u>discrimination</u> because she is <u>black</u> and <u>female</u>.

4) Angelou is best known for her <u>autobiographies</u>, particularly 'I Know Why the Caged Bird Sings'. It was published in 1969 and deals with her <u>childhood</u> to the age of <u>17</u>.

Angelou's poetry deals with Oppression, Ageing and Love

1) **Oppression** — Many of Angelou's poems deal with oppression based on <u>race</u>, <u>sex</u> and <u>poverty</u>, and how individuals <u>respond</u> to <u>oppression</u>, <u>loss</u> and <u>hardship</u>. She focuses on the <u>strength</u> of the <u>human spirit</u> in the face of these issues.

2) **Ageing** — Angelou's <u>first</u> book of poetry was published when she was in her <u>forties</u>, and some of her poems deal with <u>getting older</u>.

3) **Love** — Angelou deals with <u>family love</u> and <u>relationships</u> in her poetry. She writes about <u>realistic</u> love — the <u>bad</u> as well as the <u>good</u>.

Well-known poems
- On the Pulse of Morning
- Kin
- Caged Bird
- Woman Work

Her poems are meant to be Spoken Aloud

1) **Repetition** — Angelou often <u>repeats words</u>, <u>phrases</u> and sometimes <u>entire stanzas</u> in her poems. This helps to <u>emphasise</u> the point she is trying to get across. It also makes <u>parts</u> of her poems sound a bit like the <u>chorus</u> of a <u>song</u>. This makes the poem <u>sound</u> good when it's <u>read out loud</u>.

2) **Imagery** — <u>Similes</u> and <u>metaphors</u> crop up in lots of Angelou's poems. Some <u>metaphors</u> are used throughout a <u>whole poem</u> (extended metaphors).

3) **Unusual Structure** — Some of Angelou's poems have a <u>regular structure</u>, but a lot of them don't. This means she can <u>emphasise</u> words or phrases by <u>separating them</u> on a new line. It also means that her poems are <u>interesting</u> to <u>read aloud</u>.

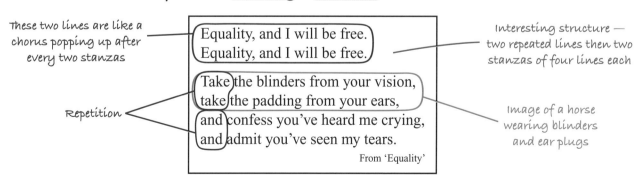

These two lines are like a chorus popping up after every two stanzas

Equality, and I will be free.
Equality, and I will be free.

Take the blinders from your vision,
take the padding from your ears,
and confess you've heard me crying,
and admit you've seen my tears.
From 'Equality'

Repetition

Interesting structure — two repeated lines then two stanzas of four lines each

Image of a horse wearing blinders and ear plugs

Angelou — "I've learned that I still have a lot to learn"...

... and so do you, about the different poets that might come up in your exam. It might seem like a lot to learn, but it'll really help in your exam if you know what themes and techniques you're looking for.

Tony Harrison

Tony Harrison (1937-present) may not speak as many <u>languages</u> as Maya Angelou, but he does know <u>Ancient Greek</u>, <u>Latin</u> and <u>Middle English</u>. None of which are spoken any more... Hmm, someone ought to tell him.

Harrison is from a Working-Class family

© REX/PETER BROOKER

1) Tony Harrison was born in <u>Leeds</u>. His dad was a baker. Harrison won a scholarship to <u>grammar school</u>, where he became fascinated by Ancient Greece. He studied <u>Classics</u> at university.

2) Harrison <u>taught English</u> at universities in Nigeria and Czechoslovakia. He moved back to the UK in 1967, determined to <u>give up teaching</u> and be a full-time <u>poet</u>.

3) As well as poetry, he writes <u>plays in verse</u> for the <u>stage</u> and <u>screen</u>, and he has <u>translated</u> classic texts from Ancient Greek, Middle English and French.

4) In 1995 the Guardian newspaper sent him to <u>Bosnia</u>, where he wrote poems from the <u>front line</u> of the <u>war</u>.

His main Themes are Family, Class and Politics

1) **Family** — Harrison's <u>parents</u> didn't seem to <u>like</u> or <u>understand</u> his poetry. As Harrison became more educated in the Classics, he lost the ability to <u>connect</u> with his parents — Harrison writes about the <u>conflict</u> between him and them. However, many of his poems also focus on <u>happier</u> family <u>memories</u> and his <u>grief</u> at his parents' <u>deaths</u>.

2) **Class** — Harrison's <u>education</u> set him apart from his <u>working-class</u> roots, and he often writes about <u>divisions</u> between social classes. He is <u>critical</u> of <u>intolerance</u> and class <u>snobbery</u>.

3) **Politics** — Some of Harrison's poems reflect his views on <u>current events</u>. He speaks out against some groups enforcing their will on others based on <u>race</u>, <u>geography</u>, and <u>political</u> or <u>religious</u> views.

> **Well-known poems**
> * Them and [uz]
> * Book Ends
> * Bringing Up
> * Background Material

Harrison uses Direct Speech, Strong Rhymes and Classical Forms

1) **Direct speech** — Harrison often writes parts of a poem in his <u>parents' voice</u> by writing in a Yorkshire accent. His poems also use a lot of <u>colloquial language</u> and <u>swearing</u> to demonstrate his working-class roots.

2) **Rhyme** — Most of Harrison's poems have a <u>strict rhyme scheme</u>. This imposes <u>order</u> on complex, chaotic ideas and feelings. His poems often have a <u>regular rhythm</u> that makes them sound like <u>speech</u>.

3) **Classical forms** — Harrison often uses poetic <u>forms</u> such as sonnets and elegies, and poetic <u>techniques</u> like alliteration, but his subjects are <u>modern</u> and often <u>working class</u>. This shows that <u>human nature</u> and <u>human concerns</u> remain the same, regardless of <u>time</u>, <u>place</u> and <u>background</u>. Harrison brings together his <u>classical knowledge</u> and <u>working-class background</u> to <u>challenge</u> people's ideas of what poetry should be.

Class conflict — tugging forelock (pulling his hair) symbol of working class, but reading Greek isn't.

Alliteration.

Conflict with father — Dad wants him to have hair oil on but he doesn't want to.

> Tugging my forelock fathoming Xenophon
> grimed Greek exams with grease and lost me marks,
> so I whisper when the barber asks Owt on?
> No, thank you! YES! Dad's voice behind me barks
> From 'Still'

Regular rhythm and strict ABAB rhyme scheme.

Direct speech and northern dialect.

Class conflict — when Form 11B met 11H...

Harrison's poems aren't all that easy to get your head round, but conflict and divisions between different groups of people come up in most of them. Look for hints of that as a starting point.

Wendy Cope

Wendy Cope (1945-present) was born in Stratford-upon-Avon in the <u>sixteenth century</u>, wrote some of the most <u>famous plays</u> in the English language and... oh, hang on, that's <u>Shakespeare</u>. Here's some stuff about Cope...

Cope has worked as a Teacher, Critic and Poet

1) Wendy Cope was born and brought up in <u>Kent</u>. She trained as a <u>teacher</u>, and taught in <u>primary schools</u> for fifteen years before becoming a <u>professional writer</u>.

2) She worked as an <u>editor</u> and a <u>TV critic</u>, then became a full-time <u>poet</u>. Her first volume of poetry was a huge <u>success</u>, and she became famous overnight. She was even favourite to be <u>Poet Laureate</u> at one point, but she refused to consider it.

3) She sometimes writes about the <u>small</u>, <u>mundane</u> details of life. However, lots of her poems also deal with <u>serious subjects</u>, but in a <u>light-hearted</u> way.

She often writes about Relationships, Writing and Family

1) **Relationships** — Cope writes about all the <u>stages</u> of a relationship, from trying to <u>meet someone</u> to <u>breaking up</u>. Lots of her early poems are quite <u>cynical</u> — they're <u>light-hearted</u> in tone, but they're often about being <u>single</u> and <u>lonely</u>. Her later poems are much <u>happier</u>.

2) **Writing** — Some of Cope's poems are about the <u>process</u> of writing a poem, or are <u>responses</u> to <u>criticisms</u> of her work.

3) **Family** — Cope's poems about her <u>parents</u> focus on her feeling of <u>not being good enough</u>. She writes more <u>warmly</u> about her <u>grandma</u>, but her poems have an air of <u>regret</u>.

Well-known poems
- Flowers
- Spared
- Names
- If I Don't Know
- Faint Praise
- After the Lunch

Her poems are Direct, Funny and often use Traditional Forms

1) **Directness** — Cope tends to use <u>straightforward vocabulary</u> and <u>short sentences</u>. This makes her poems easy to read, and means that her <u>message</u> often comes across strongly. She often writes in the <u>first person</u> (using 'I' or 'me') which makes her poems seem <u>personal</u>.

2) **Humour** — Cope often uses <u>humour</u> to make <u>serious points</u>, and to put sad situations into <u>perspective</u>. She often <u>parodies</u> (makes fun of) other well-known poets, including Wordsworth and T.S. Eliot.

3) **Form** — Wendy Cope's poems generally have a strong <u>rhyme scheme</u>, and often have a specific <u>form</u>, such as a <u>sonnet</u>, <u>triolet</u> (an eight line poem with a specific rhyme scheme) or <u>haiku</u>. This can make her poems seem <u>traditional</u> at first glance, but the content of her poems is often the <u>opposite</u> of what you might expect.

This extract is from a sonnet, which is often a love poem. This makes the subject matter unexpected.

First person narrator makes it direct.

Small men can be aggressive, people say,
But you are often genial and kind,
As long as you can have things all your way
And I comply, and do not speak my mind
From 'Faint Praise'

Simple vocabulary and syntax. Chatty tone.

Strong ABAB rhyme scheme.

"It's such a mess!" — woman's horror over custard pie fight... *

Bizarrely, Wendy Cope sometimes writes as a man called Jason Strugnell, who's a struggling poet. It's not very likely that "Strugnell's" poems will come up in the exam, but they're still worth a read.

* Unlike Cope, I like to deal with light-hearted subjects in a serious way.

Brian Patten

Brian Patten (1946-present) writes poetry that works well when it's <u>performed</u> (read out loud). He aims to write poems that appeal to a <u>wide range</u> of people, not just people who like <u>traditional</u> types of poetry.

Patten writes for *Adults* and *Children*

© Jeff Morgan 06 / Alamy

1) Patten grew up in <u>Liverpool</u>. He left school at <u>15</u> and became a <u>reporter</u>.

2) He became <u>famous</u> in 1967 when he published a <u>book of poems</u> called 'The Mersey Sound' along with two other poets from <u>Liverpool</u>. They became known as the <u>Liverpool Poets</u>, and had strong links to <u>pop music</u> and poetry as <u>performance</u>.

3) Since then, Patten has published several collections of his <u>own poems</u>. His poems are aimed at <u>children</u> as well as <u>adults</u>. He's also published <u>story books</u> for children and edited two <u>collections</u> of poetry.

His main *Themes* are *Love, Death, Growing up* and *Nature*

1) **Love** — Patten's poems deal with <u>all sides of love</u>, from <u>new relationships</u>, to <u>break-ups</u>, to the love he feels for his <u>mother</u> and his <u>friends</u>.

2) **Death** — He writes about the fact that <u>death</u> is waiting for everyone and can't be <u>avoided</u>. He also writes about how hard it is to be <u>left behind</u> when other people die.

3) **Growing up** — Many of Patten's poems deal with what it's <u>like</u> to be a <u>child</u>, and the <u>sadness</u> of having to <u>grow up</u>. A lot of his poems are about using your <u>imagination</u> — an ability that adults tend to lose.

Well-known poems
• So Many Different Lengths of Time
• A Blade of Grass
• Staring at the Crowd
• A Small Dragon

4) **Nature** — He also writes about nature, and how the natural world can give people <u>peace</u> if they look for it.

His poems are *Direct, Immediate* and have *Interesting Rhythms*

1) **Direct** — Patten often uses the <u>first person</u> or the <u>second person</u> in his poems. This means they either describe the <u>direct feelings</u> of the <u>narrator</u>, or they're <u>addressed</u> to the <u>reader</u> as 'you'. He also often uses <u>uncomplicated language</u>, so that his meaning is <u>clear</u>.

2) **Immediate** — A lot of Patten's poems are written in the <u>present tense</u>. This helps the reader to feel <u>involved</u> in the narrator's <u>emotions</u> — they feel them at the <u>same time</u> as the narrator does.

3) **Interesting rhythms** — His poems often have <u>unusual</u> and <u>irregular rhythms</u> to vary the <u>pace</u> and <u>mood</u>, and to make them more <u>interesting</u> when they're read <u>aloud</u>.

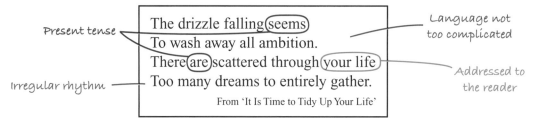

Present tense

Irregular rhythm

The drizzle falling seems
To wash away all ambition.
There are scattered through your life
Too many dreams to entirely gather.

From 'It Is Time to Tidy Up Your Life'

Language not too complicated

Addressed to the reader

I like the Patten of his poetry...

If you're studying a Brian Patten poem in class, try reading it out loud. It'll give you a sense of how the poem would sound if it was performed. Just don't try it in the exam — it'll annoy other people.

Jo Shapcott

Jo Shapcott (1953-present) is an <u>award-winning British poet</u>. She writes poems about <u>all kinds</u> of different things, but this page will give you an idea of some of the <u>main themes</u> she writes about, and her <u>writing style</u>.

Shapcott is a *Poet* and a *University Lecturer*

1) Jo Shapcott was born in <u>London</u> in 1953 and went to university in Dublin and Oxford.

2) She <u>lectures</u> in <u>creative writing</u> at a <u>university</u> in London and she published her <u>first</u> book of poetry in 1988.

3) She's won lots of <u>prizes</u> for her poetry and she won the National Poetry Competition <u>twice</u> (in 1985 and 1991).

4) In 2003, Shapcott was diagnosed with <u>cancer</u>. Her experiences of <u>illness</u> influenced the <u>themes</u> of her 2010 poetry collection 'Of Mutability'.

© REX/Nick Cunard

Her *Themes include Science, Nature and Everyday Life*

1) **Science** — Shapcott writes about how <u>advances in science</u> change the way we think about <u>life</u> and about <u>ourselves</u>. Her experience of <u>illness</u> may have heightened her interest in this theme.

2) **Nature** — Many of Shapcott's poems are about <u>nature</u>. She writes about the effect <u>humanity</u> has on the <u>natural world</u>, and the effect the <u>natural world</u> has on <u>humanity</u>.

3) **Everyday Life** — Shapcott observes <u>little things</u> about <u>everyday life</u> and puts them into her poetry — for example she's written about a <u>mug</u> and a <u>shopping trip</u>. Writing about these everyday things allows her to make a comment about something more <u>universal</u>, but keeps her poems easy to <u>relate</u> to.

Well-known poems
- Of Mutability
- Phrase Book
- Electroplating the Baby
- The Mad Cow Talks Back

She uses *Characters, Images and Free Verse*

1) **Characters** — Shapcott's poems are often written about different <u>characters</u> — <u>people</u>, <u>animals</u>, or even a <u>lettuce</u>. This means her poems often have a <u>narrative</u>, and makes her books of poems really <u>varied</u> and <u>interesting</u> for her readers.

2) **Imagery** — She uses imagery like <u>similes</u>, <u>metaphors</u> and <u>personification</u> to bring her poems to life. These images are often quite <u>humorous</u> or <u>unusual</u>.

3) **Free Verse** — Most of her poems <u>don't rhyme</u>, they don't really have a <u>strict rhythm</u> and often the stanzas aren't <u>even lengths</u>.

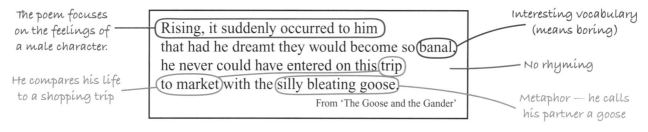

The poem focuses on the feelings of a male character.

He compares his life to a shopping trip

Rising, it suddenly occurred to him
that had he dreamt they would become so banal,
he never could have entered on this trip
to market with the silly bleating goose.

From 'The Goose and the Gander'

Interesting vocabulary (means boring)

No rhyming

Metaphor — he calls his partner a goose

I've written you a little poem...

It's called 'Exams' and it goes like this. 'Exams are a part of everyday life. They cause people lots of trouble and strife. To make them easier, do some revision — don't be tempted to watch television.'

Sophie Hannah

Sophie Hannah (1971-present) is the <u>second to last</u> of the poets who could come up in your exam.
Just for you, here's a <u>whole page</u> about her.

Sophie Hannah writes *Poetry* and *Crime Novels*

© REX/Geoffrey Swaine

1) Sophie Hannah was born in <u>Manchester</u> and now lives in <u>Cambridge</u> with her husband and two children.

2) She published her <u>first</u> collection of <u>poetry</u> in 1995, when she was 24.

3) As well as poetry, she has written <u>crime</u> fiction, <u>short stories</u> and a book for <u>children</u>. Some of her crime novels have been made into <u>TV dramas</u>.

She writes about *Relationships* and *People*

1) **Relationships** — Lots of Hannah's poems are about <u>relationships</u> between men and women, particularly <u>affairs</u> and <u>romantic</u> relationships that have <u>failed</u>, or are failing. The <u>tone</u> of these poems is often quite <u>bitter</u>, but also humorous, focusing on the other person's <u>faults</u>.

2) **Human Behaviour** — Hannah often <u>pokes fun</u> at the way people (herself included) <u>act</u>, particularly <u>experts</u> (e.g. doctors and therapists) and <u>rule-makers</u> (e.g. local councils). She finds <u>humour</u> in <u>everyday life</u>.

3) **Human Failings** — Lots of Hannah's poems pick out other people's perceived <u>faults</u>. She sometimes portrays <u>men</u> as <u>stubborn</u> or <u>weak</u>, and other <u>women</u> as <u>dishonest</u> or <u>judgemental</u>.

Well-known poems
- **Person Specification**
- **'No Ball Games etc'**
- **Hotels Like Houses**
- **Your Dad Did What?**
- **Pessimism for Beginners**

She uses a *First-Person Voice* and lots of *Poetic Techniques*

1) **First/second person voice** — Hannah tends to write in the <u>first</u> or <u>second person</u> (e.g. using 'I' and 'you'). Her relationship poems are often <u>addressed</u> to her partner, and usually <u>tell a story</u>. This makes them seem <u>direct</u> and <u>personal</u>.

2) **Form** — Hannah often uses traditional <u>forms</u>, most commonly <u>sonnets</u>, but her content is <u>not traditional</u>. Most of her poems have a <u>strong rhyme scheme</u> and <u>short lines</u>. This gives them a <u>jaunty</u>, <u>upbeat rhythm</u>, which makes them easy to read and adds to their <u>humour</u>.

3) **Techniques** — She uses various <u>techniques</u> to emphasise particular ideas. She often uses <u>repetition</u> and <u>alliteration</u> to highlight a key theme, <u>exaggeration</u> to make things seem <u>ridiculous</u>, <u>enjambment</u> to stress particular words or finish a rhyme and <u>caesura</u> to interrupt the rhythm of the poem or separate ideas.

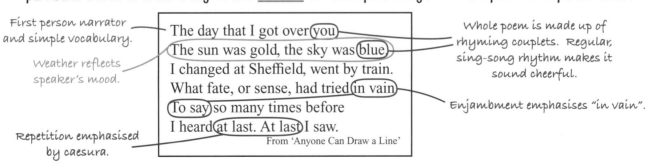

First person narrator and simple vocabulary.

Weather reflects speaker's mood.

Repetition emphasised by caesura.

The day that I got over you
The sun was gold, the sky was blue.
I changed at Sheffield, went by train.
What fate, or sense, had tried in vain
To say so many times before
I heard at last. At last I saw.

From 'Anyone Can Draw a Line'

Whole poem is made up of rhyming couplets. Regular, sing-song rhythm makes it sound cheerful.

Enjambment emphasises "in vain".

Dead Poets Society — where poetry meets crime...

I'm not sure that Sophie Hannah's love of crime writing comes across in her poetry. Which is probably just as well — given how angry she seems to get, most of her poems could easily end in murder.

Owen Sheers

Owen Sheers (1974-present) is the only poet on the list who's been the official writer for a rugby team.
I was the official writer for my local abseiling club — until they let me go. But that's enough about me...

Sheers has written Poetry, Prose and Drama

1) Owen Sheers was born in Fiji, but grew up in South Wales.

2) As well as poetry, he has written fiction, non-fiction, plays and journalistic pieces.
His first novel, 'Resistance', was made into a film.

3) He's also done a bit of acting and presented some programmes for the BBC.

4) He was the writer in residence for the Welsh Rugby Union in 2012.

© REX/Geoffrey Swaine

Sheers writes about some Big Themes

1) `Man vs. nature` — Lots of Sheers' poems are influenced by the Welsh countryside. He writes about how
people interact with the environment, and leave their mark on the landscape. He also writes about the
landscape as a record of history, that can be read like a book — once man has gone, only nature remains.

2) `Separation` — Sheers also writes a lot of about different kinds of separation. Quite a few of his poems
deal with the breakdown of relationships, others with the death of family members.

3) `Growing up` — Several of Sheers' poems focus on the loss of innocence that
comes with growing up. In these poems, Sheers sometimes refers to the circularity
of life, and the idea that an ending (of life or a relationship) is also a beginning.

4) `War` — Sheers also writes about the unnaturalness of war, its effect on the
soldiers who fight, the people they leave behind and the places in which they fight.

Well-known poems
• Mametz Wood
• Inheritance
• On Going
• Valentine

He uses lots of Imagery and Personification

1) `Imagery` — Sheers uses natural metaphors (e.g. birds, animals and weather) to describe relationships and
feelings. He often describes things in terms of writing, for example comparing the flight of swallows to
italic text on a page. He also uses images of the theatre to highlight ideas about appearance and reality.

2) `Personification` — Places and landforms are often personified. This makes
the landscape seem more connected with the humans that live in it.

3) `Form` — Sheers doesn't use much regular rhyme, but many of his poems
have a natural rhythm. He often uses enjambment, and varies the length of his
lines or stanzas to break the flow of a poem or emphasise an idea.

Image of steadily dripping water recreates the noise of her heels. Also links the relationship to cruelty.

One-line stanza interrupts rhythm.

> The water torture of your heels
> emptying before me down that Paris street,
> evacuated as the channels of our hearts.
>
> That will be one memory.
>
> From 'Valentine'

Enjambment emphasises the word "emptying".

Poems about rugby — in a league of their own...
And that's it, the end of the information about the poets. Don't be too down-hearted though — over
the page are some poems to read and some splendid questions to help you get to grips with them.

Condolence

This section gives you loads of <u>poems</u> and some rather tasty <u>questions</u> about them. <u>Read</u> each poem, <u>annotate</u> it, then have a go at the <u>questions</u>. They're great practice for your unseen poetry exam.

This poem <u>seems</u> like it was written <u>yesterday</u>, so you might be surprised to find out that it was published in <u>1926</u>. That's the same year the <u>TV</u> was first demonstrated in public. A while ago, then.

Condolence

They hurried here, as soon as you had died,
Their faces damp with haste and sympathy,
And pressed my hand in theirs, and smoothed my knee,
And clicked their tongues, and watched me, mournful-eyed.
5   Gently they told me of that Other Side—
How, even then, you waited there for me,
And what ecstatic meeting ours would be.
Moved by the lovely tale, they broke, and cried.

And when I smiled, they told me I was brave,
10   And they rejoiced that I was comforted,
And left, to tell of all the help they gave.
But I had smiled to think how you, the dead,
So curiously preoccupied and grave,
Would laugh, could you have heard the things they said.

I smiled to think how you
would laugh could you
have seen Bald Dave sitting
in front of that plant.

Dorothy Parker

I know by now you'll be desperate to show off your poetry analysis skills, so here's your chance...
Read and annotate the poem on page 22, then have a go at answering these questions.

Q1 What is the poem about? Briefly sum up the poem's message.

Q2 Who is the poem addressing? Why has the poet written it in this way?

Q3 How do you think the narrator feels about the person who has died?

Q4 a) What do the visitors think about the afterlife?

   b) How does this compare with the narrator's view of the afterlife?

Q5 The word "and" is repeated many times in this poem. Why do you think the poet has done this?

Q6 Explain how and why the last six lines of the poem are different from the first eight lines.

Q7 Why do you think the poet chose the title "Condolence"?

Q8 The poet uses simple, matter-of-fact language. What effect does this have?

Q9 The narrator says that she "smiled" and the visitors "cried". Why is this contrast effective?

Q10 Comment on the rhythm of the poem. What effect does it have on the reader?

Now have a go at writing a proper essay for the exam-style question. Don't forget to make a plan first.

EXAM-STYLE QUESTION

What is the poet saying about the different ways that people react to death?
What methods does she use to present these ideas?

Volumes

Here's a poem that was published in <u>1992</u>. Fun Fact #35 — 1992 was <u>International Space Year</u>.
It was also the 500th anniversary of <u>Columbus's</u> first voyage to <u>America</u>. Anyway, back to <u>poetry</u>...

Volumes

They put me in a fever. It's not enough
to look. I want to hold them all
and stuff them in the gaps in my head.
I gallop past Health towards Travel
5   where I break into a muck sweat
as I lift and sniff a book about Verona.
The odour makes me stagger and long
to be a book mite, to live right inside
and gulp holes through the picture maps.
10   I don't trust myself in Fiction. The thought
of those thousands and thousands of stories —
the crush and babble of other minds —
makes the whites of my eyes show and roll.
Last time I sauntered by those shelves
15   I slammed into the New Titles display
and crashed right through a pyramid of books
on to my back among the toppled photos
of authors winking at the carry on.
I got a cuppa and a pat on the rump
20   from the kind saleslady who has the bubble
of book hysteria herself, I'd guess.
If she could, she'd wear print on her skin.
There are words written for everything,
I think, and it's only a matter of time
25   before I find a new 'How To' book:
how to stand upright, how not to fall
and how not to cry out when you do.

Jo Shapcott

You should be getting the hang of this now — read the poem, annotate the poem, answer the questions. So if you'll excuse me, I'm off for a nap. Give me a shout if you get stuck.

Q1   In one sentence, sum up what the poem is about.

Q2   Is the poem funny? Which lines seem most humorous?

Q3   What does "stuff them in the gaps in my head" mean?

Q4   How does the poet suggest that the love of books is like madness?

Q5   How does the mood of the poem change in the last five lines?

Q6   What does "the crush and babble of other minds" refer to?
      Do you think it's an effective description?

Q7   What do you think about the title of the poem? Why has the poet chosen this title?

Q8   What is the effect of using powerful verbs like "gallop", "slammed" and "crashed"?

Q9   How does the poet appeal to different senses? Give some examples and explain their effect.

Q10   Comment on the form of the poem. What effect does this have?

EXAM-STYLE QUESTION
What are the poet's feelings about books, and what methods does she use to convey these emotions?

The Sitter

This poem was published in 2001 and is written from the point of view of someone modelling for an artist. It's based on a real painting, which is kind of cool. We can imagine how the 'sitter' really felt...

The Sitter
(Vanessa Bell, *Nude*, c.1922-3, Tate Britain)

Depressed and disagreeable and fat —
That's how she saw me. It was all she saw.
Around her, yes, I may have looked like that.
She hardly spoke. She thought I was a bore.
5   Beneath her gaze I couldn't help but slouch.
She made me feel ashamed. My face went red.
I'd rather have been posing on a couch
For some old rake who wanted me in bed.
Some people made me smile, they made me shine,
10   They made me beautiful. But they're all gone,
Those friends, the way they saw this face of mine,
And her contempt for me is what lives on.
Admired, well-bred, artistic Mrs Bell,
I hope you're looking hideous in Hell.

POEM DICTIONARY
rake — a womanizer

Rover just didn't think
the photographer had
captured his good side.

Wendy Cope

Oooh, that was so <u>awkward</u>. I don't think the narrator really <u>liked</u> her painting. If you've ever seen the painting she's talking about, you'll <u>understand why</u> — it's not exactly flattering...

Q1   In one sentence, sum up what you think the main message of the poem is.

Q2   What attitude do you think the painter has towards her model?

Q3   How does the mood of the poem change in lines 9-11?

Q4   What do you think the narrator means by "her contempt for me is what lives on"?

Q5   Why do you think the narrator would rather be "posing on a couch / For some old rake who wanted me in bed"?

Q6   The poem uses simple language and short sentences. Why do you think this is?

Q7   The poem is a sonnet, a form often used for love poems. Why do you think the poet chose this form?

Q8   Find an example of repetition in the poem and explain what effect it has.

Q9   Do you think the first line of the poem is effective? Explain your answer.

Q10   What do you notice about the final two lines of the poem? What effect does this have?

EXAM-STYLE QUESTION

What do you think the poet is saying about the difference between art and reality? How does she use poetic techniques to present these ideas?

The Dead-Beat

Wilfred Owen wrote this poem during the First World War, so don't go expecting it to be full of rainbows and rays of sunshine. I'll warn you, it's pretty bleak, but it's definitely worth a read...

The Dead-Beat

He dropped, – more sullenly than wearily,
Lay stupid like a cod, heavy like meat,
And none of us could kick him to his feet;
– Just blinked at my revolver, blearily;
5   – Didn't appear to know a war was on,
Or see the blasted trench at which he stared.
'I'll do 'em in,' he whined. 'If this hand's spared,
I'll murder them, I will.'
                A low voice said,
'It's Blighty, p'raps, he sees; his pluck's all gone,
10   Dreaming of all the valiant, that *aren't* dead:
Bold uncles, smiling ministerially;
Maybe his brave young wife, getting her fun
In some new home, improved materially.
It's not these stiffs have crazed him; nor the Hun.'

15   We sent him down at last, out of the way.
Unwounded; – stout lad, too, before that strafe.
Malingering? Stretcher-bearers winked, 'Not half!'

Next day I heard the Doc's well-whiskied laugh:
'That scum you sent last night soon died. Hooray!'

POEM DICTIONARY
Blighty — a nickname for Britain
pluck — courage
ministerially — like a church minister
stiffs — dead bodies
Hun — a nickname for German soldiers (the enemy)
malingering — to fake or exaggerate an illness to get out of something

Wilfred Owen

I'm sure you're eager for <u>more</u> questions by now, and it's your lucky day... Here are some questions about the poem on page 30 — have a good <u>read</u> of the poem before you <u>answer</u> them.

Q1   Write down what you think the poem is about, in just one sentence.

Q2   Why do you think the poet compares the man to "a cod" and "meat"?

Q3   People try to "kick him to his feet". What does this show about life in the trenches?

Q4   How do the medical staff react to the patient? What do you think about their reactions?

Q5   The poem ends in the word "Hooray!". What effect does this have?

Q6   What do you think of the title of this poem? Why do you think the poet chose this title?

Q7   The poet uses direct speech in this poem. What effect does this have on the reader?

Q8   What do you notice about the rhyme scheme of the poem? What effect does this have?

Q9   The words "Unwounded" and "Malingering" are separated from the rest
      of their lines by punctuation. Why do you think the poet has done this?

Q10   Wilfred Owen felt sympathy for soldiers who had breakdowns during the war.
      How does the attitude of the narrator differ from this view?

EXAM-STYLE QUESTION

> What is the poet saying about the nature of war,
> and how does he convey this to the reader?

The Tyger

This poem was published in <u>1794</u>, so it's the <u>oldest</u> poem in this section. Blake actually <u>illustrated</u> the original version of this poem himself. He drew a big picture of a <u>tiger</u> at the bottom — lovely.

The Tyger

Tyger! Tyger! burning bright
In the forests of the night,
What immortal hand or eye
Could frame thy fearful symmetry?

5   In what distant deeps or skies
Burnt the fire of thine eyes?
On what wings dare he aspire?
What the hand dare seize the fire?

And what shoulder, and what art,
10   Could twist the sinews of thy heart?
And when thy heart began to beat,
What dread hand? and what dread feet?

What the hammer? what the chain?
In what furnace was thy brain?
15   What the anvil? what dread grasp
Dare its deadly terrors clasp?

When the stars threw down their spears,
And water'd heaven with their tears,
Did he smile his work to see?
20   Did he who made the Lamb make thee?

Tyger! Tyger! burning bright
In the forests of the night,
What immortal hand or eye,
Dare frame thy fearful symmetry?

<u>POEM DICTIONARY</u>
frame — design or create
aspire — to strive towards an achievement
sinews — tendons or muscles
dread — frightening and awe-inspiring

William Blake

Your next mission, should you choose to accept it, is to have a good <u>read</u> of the poem on page 32, <u>annotate</u> the most important bits, then have a go at <u>answering</u> these questions.

Q1   Briefly explain what you think the poem is about.

Q2   What attitude do you think the narrator has towards the tiger?

Q3   Why does the narrator describe the tiger as "burning bright"? What do you think this means?

Q4   Why do you think the poet only mentions some parts of the tiger's creator, like the "hand" and "eye"?

Q5   The poem is made up almost entirely of questions. What effect does this have?

Q6   Give one example of alliteration in the poem. What does the alliteration achieve?

Q7   Which of the images in the poem do you think is the most effective? Explain your answer.

Q8   Comment on the rhythm of the poem. What effect does this have on the reader?

Q9   Why does the poet ask "Did he who made the Lamb make thee?"

Q10 a)   Why does the poet repeat the first stanza at the end of the poem?

    b)   Why does he replace the word "Could" with "Dare"?

> **EXAM-STYLE QUESTION**
> What do you think the poem is about, and how does it achieve
> its effects through imagery and the language chosen?

Jumper

This poem was published in the <u>1970s</u>, but part of it is a memory from the 1940s, during <u>World War Two</u>. During the war, UK cities were often <u>bombed</u>, so people hid inside bomb shelters for <u>protection</u>.

Jumper

When I want some sort of human metronome
to beat calm celebration out of fear
like that when German bombs fell round our home
it's my mother's needles, knitting, that I hear,
5   the click of needles steady though walls shake.
The stitches, plain or purl, were never dropped.
Bombs fell all that night until daybreak
but, not for a moment, did the knitting stop.
Though we shivered in the cellar-shelter's cold
10   and the whistling bombs sent shivers through the walls
I know now why she made her scared child hold
the skeins she wound so calmly into balls.

We open presents wrapped before she died.
With that same composure shown in that attack
15   she'd known the time to lay her wools aside —

the jumper I open 's shop-bought, and is black!

<u>POEM DICTIONARY</u>
metronome — a machine that ticks at a constant speed to help musicians stay in time
plain and purl — types of stitch in knitting
skein — a length of wool that has been loosely twisted or coiled

Tony Harrison

Here are some more questions for you — these ones are about the poem on page 34.
Make sure you have a really good read of the poem before you answer them.

Q1   Explain briefly what you think the poem is about.

Q2   How does the poet suggest that he and his mother were in danger during the bombing?

Q3   Why do you think the narrator's mother made him hold the wool as she was knitting?

Q4   Briefly describe the emotions that the poet puts across.
       How does the poet show these emotions?

Q5   The poet uses the words "shivered" and "shivers" on consecutive lines. What effect does this have?

Q6 a) How are the last four lines of the poem different from the first twelve lines?

   b) Why do you think the poet has done this?

Q7   How does the poet use the senses in the poem? Do you think this is effective?

Q8   Find an example of onomatopoeia in the poem and explain its effect.

Q9   What do you notice about the rhythm of the poem? What effect does this have?

Q10   Why do you think it is significant that the jumper is "shop-bought" and "black"?
       Why has this description been separated from the rest of the stanza?

EXAM-STYLE QUESTION

What does the poem suggest about the nature of courage?
How does the poet present these ideas?

History

Here's a poem about <u>Wales</u> that was published in <u>2005</u>. I love Wales. It rains a bit sometimes, but who doesn't like a bit of rain? You don't? Oh. Well hopefully you'll like the <u>poem</u> anyway.

History
Lledr Valley, North Wales

Don't try to learn this place
in the pages of a history
but go instead up to the
disused quarry

5   where the water lies still
and black as oil
and the only chiselling
is that of the blackbird's song

     drilling its notes
10   into the hillside's soil.

And there, beside the falls of moss,
pick yourself a blade of slate,
long as your arm, rusted,
metallic in sound.

15   Tap it with your heel,
then with your fingertips
at its leaves, gently
prise it apart.

And see how it becomes
20   a book of slate

in which you can read
a story of stone —
one that's written
throughout this valley,

25   in every head, across every heart
and down the marrow of every bone.

Owen Sheers

And now for something <u>completely different</u> — don your tweed jacket, get your magnifying glass and meet me in the drawing room... Oops, sorry, my mistake, it's actually time for some more <u>questions</u>.

Q1   What is the poem about? Try to sum up the theme or message in one sentence.

Q2   The narrator describes the quarry as "disused". Find another description which suggests that people used to work there.

Q3   Describe the mood of the poem.

Q4   How do you think the narrator feels about the place he is describing? How can you tell?

Q5   Find an example of consonance in this poem and say why it is effective.

Q6   What is the main image in the poem? Why is it effective?

Q7   Find one example of rhyme in the poem. What effect does this have?

Q8   What do you notice about the poet's use of sentences? How effective is this?

Q9   The poem gives the reader instructions. Why do you think the poet has done this?

Q10   Why are the final two lines of the poem particularly effective?

EXAM-STYLE QUESTION

What do you think the poet is saying about the relationship between man and nature? How does he present his ideas?

On the Grasshopper and Cricket

Rumour has it that Keats had a <u>contest</u> with a friend in 1816 to see who could write the <u>best sonnet</u> about grasshoppers and crickets. This poem was the <u>result</u>, and it's not too shabby, considering.

On the Grasshopper and Cricket

The poetry of earth is never dead:
When all the birds are faint with the hot sun,
And hide in cooling trees, a voice will run
From hedge to hedge about the new-mown mead;
5   That is the Grasshopper's – he takes the lead
In summer luxury, – he has never done
With his delights; for when tired out with fun
He rests at ease beneath some pleasant weed.
The poetry of earth is ceasing never:
10   On a lone winter evening, when the frost
Has wrought a silence, from the stove there shrills
The Cricket's song, in warmth increasing ever,
And seems to one in drowsiness half lost,
The Grasshopper's among some grassy hills.

<u>POEM DICTIONARY</u>
mead — grassland or meadow

Coincidentally, cricket was the
Cricket's favourite winter sport.

John Keats

Before you answer these questions, <u>read</u> the poem all the way through <u>slowly</u>.
Then read it again and <u>underline</u> the bits that stand out to you.

Q1   In one sentence, describe what you think the poem is about.

Q2   Briefly describe the mood of the poem.

Q3   What do you think the poet means by "when the frost / Has wrought a silence"?

Q4   Sonnets like this one are traditionally about love.
       Why do you think the poet chose this form of poem?

Q5   Keats repeats the phrase "The poetry of earth". What effect does this have?

Q6   Why do you think the poet has capitalised "Grasshopper" and "Cricket"?

Q7   What do you notice about the rhythm of the poem? What effect does this have?

Q8   What do you notice about the rhyme scheme of the poem? Why has the poet used this scheme?

Q9   The poet sometimes writes words in an unusual order. Find an example and explain its effect.

Q10 a) What do you think the Grasshopper represents?

    b) Why do you think the poet mentions the Grasshopper at the end of the poem?

EXAM-STYLE QUESTION

What do you think the poet is saying about the seasons?
Explain how he presents these ideas.

The More Loving One

Auden wrote this poem in 1957, so officially it's modern, although it might not seem like it...
Well, it's modern compared to a horse-drawn carriage, but old-fashioned compared to a smartphone.

The More Loving One

Looking up at the stars, I know quite well
That, for all they care, I can go to hell,
But on earth indifference is the least
We have to dread from man or beast.

5   How should we like it were stars to burn
With a passion for us we could not return?
If equal affection cannot be,
Let the more loving one be me.

Admirer as I think I am
10   Of stars that do not give a damn,
I cannot, now I see them, say
I missed one terribly all day.

Were all stars to disappear or die,
I should learn to look at an empty sky
15   And feel its total dark sublime,
Though this might take me a little time.

Nope, they couldn't care
less about any of us.

W. H. Auden

This is definitely a <u>tricky</u> poem to get your head round, so sorry about that. If you're a bit confused, have <u>an extra read</u> through it before you dive into these <u>questions</u>.

Q1   What do you think the poem is about? Briefly explain your opinion.

Q2   What is meant by "indifference is the least / We have to dread from man or beast"?

Q3   What do you think the stars represent? Explain your answer.

Q4   Comment on the poet's use of personification in the poem. What effect does it have?

Q5   What is the mood of the poem?

Q6   Give two examples of alliteration in the poem. What effect do they have?

Q7   What effect do strong phrases like "go to hell" and "give a damn" have on the reader?

Q8   What is the rhyme scheme of this poem and why do you think the poet chose it?

Q9   Find an example of enjambment in the poem. What effect does it have?

Q10   Why do you think the last line of the poem is so effective?

EXAM-STYLE QUESTION

> What do you think the poet is saying about love
> and how does he use imagery to convey his ideas?

Winter: My Secret

Rossetti published this poem in 1862 so it's not exactly cutting edge. But if you've ever tried to keep a secret from someone who really really wants to know it then you'll know where she's coming from.

Winter: My Secret

I tell my secret? No indeed, not I:
Perhaps some day, who knows?
But not today; it froze, and blows, and snows
And you're too curious: fie!
5   You want to hear it? well:
Only, my secret's mine, and I won't tell.

Or, after all, perhaps there's none:
Suppose there is no secret after all,
But only just my fun.
10   Today's a nipping day, a biting day;
In which one wants a shawl,
A veil, a cloak, and other wraps:
I cannot ope to every one who taps,
And let the draughts come whistling through my hall;
15   Come bounding and surrounding me,
Come buffeting, astounding me,
Nipping and clipping through my wraps and all.
I wear my mask for warmth: who ever shows
His nose to Russian snows
20   To be pecked at by every wind that blows?
You would not peck? I thank you for your good will,
Believe, but leave the truth untested still.

Spring's an expansive time: yet I don't trust
March with its peck of dust,
25   Nor April with its rainbow-crowned brief showers,
Nor even May, whose flowers
One frost may wither through the sunless hours.

Perhaps some languid summer day,
When drowsy birds sing less and less,
30   And golden fruit is ripening to excess,
If there's not much sun nor too much cloud,
And the warm wind is neither still nor loud,
Perhaps my secret I may say,
Or you may guess.

POEM DICTIONARY
ope — open
languid — lazy and relaxed

Christina Rossetti

Woo — this is it, your final set of practice questions. When you've finished these, you should be able to analyse poetry with the best of 'em, which will put you in prime position for the exam...

Q1   What was your first reaction on reading the poem, and why?

Q2   Explain briefly how the mood is different in each of the four stanzas.

Q3   Comment on the words Rossetti uses to describe winter
        (in the second stanza) and summer (in the fourth stanza).

Q4   How does the narrator use descriptions of what she is
        wearing to suggest that she is protecting her secret?

Q5   Why do you think Rossetti links keeping secrets with winter?

Q6   Why do you think the poet asks questions in this poem?

Q7   What do you notice about the last line of the poem? What effect does this have?

Q8   The rhyme scheme of the poem is irregular. Why is this effective?

Q9   The poet uses a lot of rhyme in this poem, both at the ends
        of lines, and within lines. What effect does this create?

Q10   How does Rossetti make the image of winter so powerful?

EXAM-STYLE QUESTION

What is the poet saying about keeping secrets? Paying close attention
to the imagery in the poem, explain how the poet conveys these ideas.

Exam Advice

I bet you've always wanted to be an <u>examiner</u> for the day, haven't you? Thought so. That's why I've given you <u>a whole section</u> where you can <u>mark</u> some <u>sample exam answers</u>. I knew you'd be pleased. First up, a bit of <u>general advice</u> on writing an exam answer...

You must <u>Include Quotes</u> from the poem

Each point you make must be supported by <u>evidence</u> from the poem.

1)   Put <u>exact</u> quotes inside <u>quotation marks</u> (" ") like this: ⟶   *"I believe life ends with death."*

2)   If you <u>rephrase</u> the text, you don't need quotation marks.

   E.g.   *The poet believes that life does not go on beyond death.*

3)   Try to work quotes into your sentences so that your <u>writing flows</u> nicely.

   E.g.   *The blunt, "I believe life ends with death", makes the narrator sound cold and definite.*

4)   Choose your quotes <u>carefully</u> — they must be <u>relevant</u> to the point you're making.

5)   <u>Don't</u> quote <u>large chunks</u> of text. You don't need to and it wastes time.

Your <u>Writing Style</u> <u>is</u> Important

1)   You will be marked on your <u>spelling</u>, <u>punctuation</u> and <u>grammar</u>. Write <u>formally</u>, without using slang or text speak.

2)   Think about how you present your ideas — your work needs to be <u>clear</u> and <u>easy to read</u>. Organise your answer into sensible <u>paragraphs</u> that <u>flow nicely</u>.

3)   It's a good idea to spend a few minutes <u>reading through</u> your work at the end of the exam — that way you can check it <u>makes sense</u> and <u>correct</u> any silly <u>mistakes</u>.

Your writing style is as important as your hairstyle.

This section lets you <u>Mark</u> some <u>Sample Answer Extracts</u>

1)   <u>Marking extracts</u> from sample exam answers is a <u>great way</u> to find out <u>exactly</u> what you'll need to do to get the grade you want.

2)   On the next page, I've included a <u>mark scheme</u> like the one your <u>examiners</u> will use. The idea is for <u>you</u> to use it to help you mark the sample answer extracts in the rest of the section.

3)   These extracts should give you a good idea of what the examiner will be looking for when he or she marks <u>your exam answer</u>.

4)   So before you do anything else, <u>read the mark scheme</u> and make sure you <u>understand</u> it all. You <u>won't</u> be able to do the rest of the section without it.

Mark Scheme — he's such a great guy...

This section is <u>dead useful</u>, even if I do say so myself. Don't just mark the sample answer extracts, think about what <u>you</u> would do to <u>improve</u> them — it'll help you to write a <u>better exam answer</u>.

Mark Scheme

Here's a lovely mark scheme for you to have a look at — it should give you a good idea of the sort of thing you should be doing in your answer to the Unseen Poetry question.

Use this Mark Scheme to mark the answers in this section

Look at the mark scheme below and use it to mark the sample answers in this section. This is only a rough guide to what an answer for each grade should look like, not the exact mark scheme from AQA. Speak to your teacher for more help on this. You won't get a grade — your work will be marked out of 18 — but we've given an approximate grade to show you what to aim for.

Grade	What you've written
A*	• Shows a really insightful exploration of the text • Gives original and alternative interpretation(s) of the ideas, themes and feelings in the poem • Closely analyses the details in the poem to support interpretation(s) of it • Evaluates the poet's use of language, structure and form and their effect on the reader • Shows excellent written communication, with mostly accurate spelling and grammar
A	• Really explores the text • Gives original interpretation(s) of the ideas, themes and feelings in the poem • Analyses the details of the poem to support interpretation(s) of it • Explores the poet's use of language, structure and form and their effects on the reader • Shows good written communication, with mostly accurate spelling and grammar
B	• Presents a carefully thought out response to the text • Gives a thoughtful consideration of the ideas, themes and feelings in the poem • Gives plenty of detail related to interpretation of the text • Explains how the writer has used language, structure and form and their effect on the reader • Presents information clearly, with fairly accurate spelling and grammar
C	• Gives a full response to the poem • Makes sensible comments about ideas, themes and feelings in the poems • Uses details well to support interpretation of the poem • Considers how the writer's use of language, form and structure affect the reader • Presents information clearly, but has several spelling or grammatical errors
D	• Responds to at least part of the poem • Makes general comments about the ideas, themes and feelings in the poem • Comments on things in the poem and gives some details to support the comments • Identifies the effect on the reader of the writer's choice of language, structure and form • Presentation, spelling and grammar are clear enough to get the meaning across
E	• Responds to the poem in some way • Shows awareness of ideas, themes and feelings in the poem • Comments briefly on the poem, using details to support some comments • Shows awareness of language, structure and form • Presentation, spelling and grammar are usually clear enough to get the meaning across

You can also be awarded grades F or G. We haven't included any sample answer extracts at F or G level though — so those grades aren't in this mark scheme.

Kin — Maya Angelou

Read the exam question and the poem below. Make some notes on the poem and think about how you'd answer the question. When you're ready, look at the sample answers on the next page.

> Q1   Read the poem below. What do you think the poet is saying about relationships between siblings? How does the poet present her ideas?
> (18 marks)

Kin

FOR BAILEY

We were entwined in red rings
Of blood and loneliness before
The first snows fell
Before muddy rivers seeded clouds
5   Above a virgin forest, and
Men ran naked, blue and black
Skinned into the warm embraces
Of Sheba, Eve and Lilith.
I was your sister.

10   You left me to force strangers
Into brother molds, exacting
Taxations they never
Owed or could ever pay.

You fought to die, thinking
15   In destruction lies the seed
Of birth. You may be right.

I will remember silent walks in
Southern woods and long talks
In low voices
20   Shielding meaning from the big ears
Of overcurious adults.

You may be right.
Your slow return from
Regions of terror and bloody
25   Screams, races my heart.

I hear again the laughter
Of children and see fireflies
Bursting tiny explosions in
An Arkansas twilight.

Maya Angelou

Sheba — an ancient kingdom with a famous queen
Eve — in the Bible, the first woman created by God. She leads her husband, Adam, into sin
Lilith — in Jewish folklore, a part-woman part-demon, believed by some religions to be Adam's first wife

Sample Answers

Here are some more extracts from students' sample answers. Read them, give them a grade from E to A* (have a look back at p.45 for some help), and give a few reasons why you chose that grade.

1 I like this poem becuse its about the poets brother and how much she love him and it make me think of my brother to. When she say "I will remeber silent walks in Southern woods and long talks In low voices Sheilding meaning from the big ears Of overcurios adults" it show how close her brother and her were becuse they had secretes from adults that they didnt want no-one to hear. She say "You left me" which show how he went away and maybe he died because he "fought to die" which make me feel sad. She also say how he "may be right" which mean she agree with him even tho he want to die.

a)   Write down the grade (from E to A*) you think this answer would get.

b)   Give at least two reasons why you chose that grade.

2 The poem emphasises the closeness of the two siblings, stressing how they were "entwined" long before they were born, when the forests were still "virgin" and "Men ran naked". This makes their relationship seem ancient and unchanging. The enjambment of "red rings/ Of blood" places emphasis on the word "blood", bringing to mind the saying that "blood is thicker than water". This hints that the relationship between the siblings is stronger than any relationship with friends or lovers.

However, the sense of timelessness is challenged in the second stanza, when the narrator says "You left me", and describes how she tried to "force strangers/Into brother molds", implying that she tried to replace him. But the strangers couldn't "ever pay", showing that sibling relationships are unique and irreplaceable.

a)   Write down the grade (from E to A*) you think this answer would get.

b)   Give at least two reasons why you chose that grade.

3 The poem traces the relationship of two siblings from before birth, through one of them leaving, so the other can only "remember" how close they used to be, up to the "slow return" of the one that left.

The last line of the first verse is "I was your sister." Because this is on its own line and it is a seperate sentence it seems important, which shows how vital the relationship is to the narrator. When he leaves she tries to make "strangers" take his place, showing that she can't live without her brother. Although she hates it that he "fought to die", she also says twice "You may be right", which shows that she respects him even when he has abandonned her.

At the end of the poem she says she can "hear again the laughter/Of children". The "twilight" could be a metaphor for the later years of her life, when she is looking back at how happy they were as children.

a)   Write down the grade (from E to A*) you think this answer would get.

b)   Give at least two reasons why you chose that grade.

The Armada — Brian Patten

Read the exam question and the poem below. Make some notes on the poem and think about how you'd answer the question. When you're ready, look at the sample answers on the next page.

> Q1   Read the poem below. What ideas does the poet put across about growing up?
> How does the poet present these ideas to the reader?
> (18 marks)

The Armada

      Long, long ago
when everything I was told was believable
and the little I knew was less limited than now,
I stretched belly down on the grass beside a pond
5   and to the far bank launched a child's armada.
      A broken fortress of twigs,
the paper-tissue sails of galleons,
the waterlogged branches of submarines –
all came to ruin and were on flame
10   in that dusk-red pond.
And you, mother, stood behind me,
impatient to be going,
old at twenty-three, alone,
thin overcoat flapping.
15   How closely the past shadows us.
In a hospital a mile or so from that pond
I kneel beside your bed and, closing my eyes,
reach out across the years to touch once more
that pond's cool surface,
20   and it is your cool skin I'm touching;
for as on a pond a child's paper boat
was blown out of reach
by the smallest gust of wind,
so too have you been blown out of reach
25   by the smallest whisper of death,
and a childhood memory is sharpened,
and the heart burns as that armada burnt,
long, long ago.

Brian Patten

armada — a fleet of ships, often armed

Sample Answers

Here are some more sample answers, so have another try at giving them a grade and don't forget to explain what's wrong with the answer as well as what's right.

1) The poet has happy memorys of being a child but being a grown-up is sad because his mum is older and is in hospittle. This shows that things are more compliccated when you grow up because you have to look after your parrents insted of them looking after you and this means your "heart burns" with pain.

I think the ships burning are like his mum dieing because they were both "blown out of reach". This means that he could'nt get back his boats or his mum. Also it seems like he wants to go back because he "reach out across the years".

a) Write down the grade (from E to A*) you think this answer would get.

b) Give at least two reasons why you chose that grade.

2) The poem makes growing up seem like a negative thing. Childhood is symbolised by the excitment of launching an "armada" and watching it burn, whereas adulthood is spent in a hospital, watching a loved one die. By comparing the two events, the poet shows how things that are important when your young are less so when your older.

The opening line, "Long, long ago" reminds the reader of a fairytale. Since fairytales always have a happy ending, this makes you feel safe. The poet is hinting that the problems of his childhood were managable and he knew they would be resolved. However, when this line is repeated at the end of the poem, it shows how far away the narrator's childhood is, and ends the poem on a sad note. This suggests that growing up has problems that can't be resolved.

a) Write down the grade (from E to A*) you think this answer would get.

b) Give at least two reasons why you chose that grade.

3) By comparing his mother's illness to the "ruin" of a "paper boat", the narrator highlights how the scale of the problems you encounter changes as you grow up. Just as the "armada" blew "out of reach", so his mother is passing beyond his reach. The narrator goes from lying "belly down" as a child to kneeling as an adult; this could symbolise the narrator's increasing experience and knowledge, but also the loss of stability associated with growing up.

The mother provides a contrasting view on growing up. She is described as "old at twenty-three". This may refer to the poet's view of her, showing how your percepsion of time changes as you grow older. Alternatively it may show how she has been aged by being a single parent ("alone") and by the relative poverty implied by her "thin overcoat". The fact that she is "impatient" hints that she has lost touch with childhood pleasures, perhaps through growing up too quickly. This suggests that growing up is not simply a matter of age.

a) Write down the grade (from E to A*) you think this answer would get.

b) Give at least two reasons why you chose that grade.

'I Look Into My Glass' — Thomas Hardy

Read the exam question and the poem below. Make some notes on the poem and think about how you'd answer the question. When you're ready, look at the sample answers on the next page.

Q1   Read the poem below. How does the poet feel about getting older? How does the poet present his ideas?
(18 marks)

'I Look Into My Glass'

I look into my glass,
And view my wasting skin,
And say, 'Would God it came to pass
My heart had shrunk as thin!'

5   For then, I, undistrest
By hearts grown cold to me,
Could lonely wait my endless rest
With equanimity.

But Time, to make me grieve,
10   Part steals, lets part abide;
And shakes this fragile frame at eve
With throbbings of noontide.

Thomas Hardy

undistrest — made-up word meaning 'not distressed'
equanimity — calmness
abide — remain

Darren felt pretty stupid when he realised that the angry penguin that had been following him was in fact his reflection.

Sample Answers

Here are some more extracts from sample answers for you to read and award with a grade from E to A*. (Now might be a good time to remind yourself of the mark scheme on page 45.)

① The poet is not happy about getting older and you can tell this from the first stanzer when he looks into the mirror and says he can see his "wasting skin". He thinks that people are begginning to care less about him as he gets older and it would be good if he didn't care; and could just wait to die. In the last stanzer he explains that he still needs to be loved even though his body is a "fragile frame". The poet uses personfication to make Time seem like a thief who has taken away his looks and left his feelings. The "throbbings of noontide" are the feelings he had when he was younger, and still has now. They sound quite violent compared to the way he describes his feeble body now.

    a)   **Write down the grade (from E to A*) you think this answer would get.**

    b)   **Give at least two reasons why you chose that grade.**

② The poet views ageing in a negative light, regarding youthful good looks as something that time "steals". He uses the heart as a metaphor for his emotions, and wishes that it "had shrunk as thin" as his skin, so that he would be "undistrest" by people no longer loving him.

The alliteration on "fragile frame" highlights how frail he has become, making the reader feel his pain and agree with him that it is not fair that old people are still troubled by the same feelings as the young (the "throbbings of noontide"). By personifying time as a thief, the poet makes it sound like an enemy, who wants to "make [him] grieve". This shows that ageing and the passing of time are bad.

    a)   **Write down the grade (from E to A*) you think this answer would get.**

    b)   **Give at least two reasons why you chose that grade.**

③ The poem describes the feelings of a man on seeing his reflection. His "wasting skin" symbolises his decline towards death. However, the irony the narrator observes is that, despite his physical wastage, his "heart" (symbolising his feelings) remains unchanged, meaning that he feels the full force of "hearts grown cold". This could mean people who have ceased to love him as he grows older or, taken more literally, loved ones who have died.

The regular rhythm of the poem, achieved by the use of a strong ABAB rhyme scheme, brings to mind the beating of a heart. This reinforces Hardy's message that the "throbbings" of emotion are just as potent in later years as at "noontide". This encourages the reader to view ageing as superficial, and to understand that old people retain the same qualities they had when younger.

    a)   **Write down the grade (from E to A*) you think this answer would get.**

    b)   **Give at least two reasons why you chose that grade.**

Don't Say I Said — Sophie Hannah

Read the exam question and the poem below. Make some notes on the poem and think about how you'd answer the question. When you're ready, look at the sample answers on the next page.

> Q1   Read the poem below. What do you think the poet is saying about the way people react when a relationship has ended? How does the poet convey her ideas?
> (18 marks)

Don't Say I Said

Next time you speak to you-know-who
I've got a message for him.
Tell him that I have lost a stone
Since the last time I saw him.
5   Tell him that I've got three new books
Coming out soon, but play it
Cool, make it sound spontaneous.
Don't say I said to say it.

He might ask if I've mentioned him.
10   Say I have once, in passing.
Memorize everything he says
And, no, it won't be grassing
When you repeat his words to me –
It's the only way to play it.
15   Tell him I'm toned and tanned and fine.
Don't say I said to say it.

Say that serenity and grace
Have taken root inside me.
My top-note is frivolity
20   But beneath, dark passions guide me.
Tell him I'm radiant and replete
And add that every day it
Seems I am harder to resist.
Don't say I said to say it.

25   Tell him that all my ancient faults
Have been eradicated.
I do not carp or analyse
As I might have when we dated.
Say I'm not bossy any more
30   Or, better still, convey it
Subtly, but get the point across.
Don't say I said to say it.

"On second thoughts, you don't
need to tell him how cool I am.
Just show him this photo."

Sophie Hannah

Sample Answers

Last chance for you to use your sound sense of judgement to mark sample answers.
Then you can take that examiner's hat off, safe in the knowledge that you know what they're after when you tackle the Unseen Poetry question.

① In the poem, the narrator obsessively instructs a friend in exactly what information to pass on to an ex-partner: "Tell him I'm radiant". The speaker's need to "play it/Cool" creates irony: she is desperate for her former partner to know how well she is doing, but equally desperate for him not to know that she wants to impress him. This is highlighted by the refrain "Don't say I said to say it", which sounds forced and unnatural, much like the image she wants to present.

The poem is written as a monologue; the end-stopped double rhymes (e.g. "play it."/"say it.") on the odd lines increase the pace of the poem, giving the impression that there is no opportunity for the listener to speak. This, together with the repetition of "I", illustrates the egotism that follows the breakdown of the relationship. The speaker pays no attention to whether her friend is comfortable lying for her (e.g. the ironic order "Say I'm not bossy any more") or "repeat[ing] his words". This shows how the breakdown of a relationship can result in a war zone, where one or both parties try to make mutual friends take sides.

a)   Write down the grade (from E to A*) you think this answer would get.

b)   Give at least two reasons why you chose that grade.

② The narrator seems to still be in love with her ex, this is shown by all the things she wants her friend to say to impress him, e.g. "I'm toned and tanned and fit". This suggests that he ended the relationship, and she wants him to know that she has changed and all her "faults/Have been eradicated". This shows how often, when a relationship ends, one person wants it to carry on and will say or do anything to get back together.

She uses a technique called injament to emphasise words like "Cool" and "Subtly" to show how she wants her friend to act. By telling her friend exactly how to act she shows that she's bossy, even though she says "I'm not bossy any more". This shows that she hasn't really changed, so she hasn't learned anything from being dumped.

a)   Write down the grade (from E to A*) you think this answer would get.

b)   Give at least two reasons why you chose that grade.

③ The form of the poem mimics the content: on the surface it seems light and playful, but the careful rhymes (e.g. "inside me"/"guide me") reveal how much the narrator cares. This highlights that, while she wants to appear "replete" without her ex-partner, he is still a central part of her life. Similarly, the somewhat awkward rhythm of the poem, created by the forced rhymes and enjambment of lines such as "And add that every day it/Seems I am harder to resist", emphasises the fact that her desperation to come across well makes her clumsy and awkward. This shows how the breakdown of a relationship can bring out the worst in people.

a)   Write down the grade (from E to A*) you think this answer would get.

b)   Give at least two reasons why you chose that grade.

Long Distance II — Tony Harrison

This section is full of unseen poetry questions <u>exactly</u> like the one you'll get in the <u>exam</u>. Give yourself <u>thirty minutes</u> to do each one. Don't forget to <u>analyse</u> the poem, make an <u>essay plan</u> and then get <u>writing</u>.

This question is set out as a Foundation tier question, but you can still answer it if you're doing Higher. The rest of the questions in this section are set out as Higher tier questions, but you can still answer them if you're doing Foundation.

Q1   Read the poem below, then answer both parts **a)** and **b)**.

    a)   How do you think the poet feels about his father's behaviour after his mother's death?

    b)   How does the poet present his feelings in the poem?   (18 marks)

Spend about 30 minutes answering each of the questions in this section — that's roughly how long you'll have in the exam.

Long Distance II

Though my mother was already two years dead
Dad kept her slippers warming by the gas,
put hot water bottles her side of the bed
and still went to renew her transport pass.

5   You couldn't just drop in. You had to phone.
He'd put you off an hour to give him time
to clear away her things and look alone
as though his still raw love were such a crime.

He couldn't risk my blight of disbelief
though sure that very soon he'd hear her key
10   scrape in the rusted lock and end his grief.
He *knew* she'd just popped out to get the tea.

I believe life ends with death, and that is all.
You haven't both gone shopping; just the same,
in my new black leather phone book there's your name
15   and the disconnected number I still call.

Tony Harrison

blight — a disease that damages or destroys the thing it affects

The Send-Off — Wilfred Owen

Q1   Read the poem below. What do you think the poet is saying about
      sending men to war? How does the poet present his ideas?
      (18 marks)

The Send-Off

Down the close darkening lanes they sang their way
To the siding-shed,
And lined the train with faces grimly gay.

Their breasts were stuck all white with wreath and spray
5   As men's are, dead.

Dull porters watched them, and a casual tramp
Stood staring hard,
Sorry to miss them from the upland camp.

Then, unmoved, signals nodded, and a lamp
10   Winked to the guard.

So secretly, like wrongs hushed-up, they went.
They were not ours:
We never heard to which front these were sent;

Nor there if they yet mock what women meant
15   Who gave them flowers.

Shall they return to beatings of great bells
In wild train-loads?
A few, a few, too few for drums and yells,

May creep back, silent, to village wells,
20   Up half-known roads.

Wilfred Owen

Flowers — Wendy Cope

> Q1   Read the poem below. What do you think the poet is saying about the importance
> of romance in relationships? How does the poet present her ideas?
> (18 marks)

Flowers

Some men never think of it.
You did. You'd come along
And say you'd nearly brought me flowers
But something had gone wrong.

5   The shop was closed. Or you had doubts –
The sort that minds like ours
Dream up incessantly. You thought
I might not want your flowers.

It made me smile and hug you then.
10   Now I can only smile.
But, look, the flowers you nearly brought
Have lasted all this while.

Wendy Cope

The Man He Killed — Thomas Hardy

> Q1 Read the poem below. What do you think the poet is saying about the effect of war? How does the poet present his ideas?
> (18 marks)

The Man He Killed

'Had he and I but met
By some old ancient inn,
We should have set us down to wet
Right many a nipperkin!

5   'But ranged as infantry,
And staring face to face,
I shot at him as he at me,
And killed him in his place.

'I shot him dead because –
10   Because he was my foe,
Just so: my foe of course he was:
That's clear enough; although

'He thought he'd 'list, perhaps,
Off-hand like – just as I –
15   Was out of work – had sold his traps –
No other reason why.

'Yes; quaint and curious war is!
You shoot a fellow down
You'd treat if met where any bar is,
20   Or help to half-a-crown.'

Thomas Hardy

nipperkin — half a pint or less of alcohol
'list — short for enlist, meaning to sign up for the army
traps — personal belongings
half-a-crown — an old unit of currency

Glossary

And finally, here's a handy list of terms to help you answer the unseen poetry question.
Try to use the correct word for the features in the poem — it'll help you to get top marks.

adjective	A word that describes something, e.g. "big", "fast", "annoying".
alliteration	Where words start with the same letter. It's often used in poetry to give a nice pattern to a phrase or to make it memorable. E.g. "the little I knew was less limited than now" (Patten).
ambiguity	Where a word or phrase has two or more possible meanings.
assonance	When words share the same vowel sound but the consonants are different. E.g. "trees" and "lead" in 'On the Grasshopper and Cricket' (Keats).
ballad	A form of poetry that tells a story and can often be set to music.
blank verse	Poetry written in iambic pentameter that doesn't rhyme.
caesura	A break in the rhythm of a line, often shown with punctuation marks.
colloquial	Sounding like everyday spoken language.
consonance	When words have the same consonant sounds but different vowel sounds, e.g. "years", "yours".
consonants	All the letters in the alphabet that aren't vowels.
contrast	When two things are described in a way which emphasises how different they are. E.g. A poet might contrast two different people or two different voices.
dialect	A variation of a language. People from different places or backgrounds might use different words or sentence constructions. E.g. Scottish people might say "wee" instead of "small".
elegy	A poem written to mourn the death of someone.
emotive	Something that makes you feel a particular emotion, e.g. anger, sorrow, joy.
empathy	When someone feels as if they understand what someone else is experiencing and how they feel about it.
end stopping	Finishing a line of poetry with the end of a phrase or sentence.
enjambment	When a sentence or phrase runs over from one line to the next.
euphemism	An indirect term for something upsetting or offensive, e.g. the "Other Side" is used to avoid referring directly to death in 'Condolence' (Parker).
first person	When someone talks about themself, or a group which includes them, using words like "I" and "me".
form	The type of poem and its features (rhyme, rhythm, stanza length) e.g. a sonnet, ballad, free verse.
free verse	Poetry that doesn't rhyme and has no regular rhythm.
iambic pentameter	Poetry with a metre of ten syllables — five of them stressed, and five unstressed. The stress falls on every second syllable, e.g. "Beneath her gaze I couldn't help but slouch" (Cope).
imagery	Language that creates a picture in your mind. It includes metaphors and similes.
internal rhyme	When words within a single line of a poem rhyme. E.g. "Come bounding and surrounding me" (Rossetti).
irony	When words are used in a sarcastic or comic way to imply the opposite of what they normally mean. It can also mean when there is a big difference between what people expect and what actually happens.
language	The choice of words used. Different kinds of language have different effects on the reader.
layout	The way a piece of poetry is visually presented to the reader. E.g. line length, whether the poem is broken up into different stanzas, whether lines create some kind of visual pattern.

Glossary

metaphor	A way of describing something by saying that it <u>is something else</u>, to create a vivid image. E.g. the "trip / to market" is a metaphor for the journey through life in 'The Goose and the Gander' (Shapcott).
metre	The arrangement of stressed and unstressed syllables to create <u>rhythm</u> in a line of poetry.
mood	The <u>feel</u> or <u>atmosphere</u> of a poem, e.g. humorous, threatening, eerie.
narrative	Writing that tells a <u>story</u>, e.g. the poem 'The Dead-Beat' (Owen).
narrator	The <u>voice</u> speaking the words that you're reading. E.g. a poem could be written from the point of view of a young child, which means the young child is the poem's narrator.
onomatopoeia	A word that <u>sounds like</u> the thing it's describing, e.g. "buzz", "crunch", "bang", "pop".
oxymoron	A phrase which seems to <u>contradict</u> itself because the words have opposite meanings, e.g. "loud silence".
persona	A <u>fictional character</u> or <u>identity</u> adopted by a poet. Poets often create a persona so they can describe things from a different person's <u>point of view</u>, e.g. a male poet might use a female persona.
personification	A special kind of <u>metaphor</u> where you write about something as if it's a <u>person</u> with <u>thoughts</u> and <u>feelings</u>. E.g. the stars are personified in 'The More Loving One' (Auden).
quatrain	A <u>four line</u> stanza that usually rhymes.
refrain	A <u>line</u> or <u>stanza</u> in a poem that is <u>repeated</u>, almost like the chorus of a song. E.g. the line "Equality, and I will be free" in 'Equality' by Maya Angelou.
rhyme scheme	A <u>system</u> of rhyming words in a poem, e.g. in 'The Tyger' (Blake), the <u>first</u> line of each stanza rhymes with the <u>second</u> line, and the <u>third</u> line rhymes with the <u>fourth</u> line. The <u>rhyme scheme</u> is <u>AABB</u>.
rhyming couplet	A pair of lines that are next to each other and whose final words <u>rhyme</u>.
rhythm	A pattern of sounds created by the arrangement of <u>stressed</u> and <u>unstressed</u> syllables.
second person	When the narrator talks directly to <u>another person</u> using the word "<u>you</u>".
sibilance	Repetition of "<u>s</u>" and "<u>sh</u>" sounds. E.g. "from the <u>s</u>tove there <u>sh</u>rill<u>s</u> / The Cricket'<u>s</u> <u>s</u>ong" (Keats).
simile	A way of describing something by <u>comparing</u> it to something else, usually by using the words "<u>like</u>" or "<u>as</u>". E.g. the soldier in 'The Dead-Beat' is "stupid <u>like</u> a cod" (Owen).
sonnet	A type of poem with <u>fourteen lines</u>, usually following a <u>clear rhyme scheme</u>. There are different types of sonnets. They're often on the theme of love.
stanza	A <u>group of lines</u> in a poem. Stanzas can also be called <u>verses</u>.
structure	The <u>order</u> of ideas and events, i.e. how the poem begins, develops and ends.
syllable	A single <u>unit of sound</u> within a word. E.g. "all" has one syllable, "always" has two and "establishmentarianism" has nine.
symbolism	When an object <u>stands for something else</u>. E.g. a dying flower could symbolise the end of a relationship.
theme	An <u>idea</u> or <u>topic</u> that's important in a piece of writing. E.g. A poem could be based on the theme of love.
third person	When a poem is written about <u>someone else's perspective</u> and uses words like "<u>he</u>" and "<u>she</u>".
tone	The <u>mood</u> or <u>feeling</u> suggested by the way the narrator <u>talks</u>.
voice	The <u>personality</u> narrating the poem. Poems are usually written either using the poet's voice, as if they're speaking to you <u>directly</u>, or the voice of a <u>character</u>, e.g. an elderly man.
vowels	The letters "a", "e", "i", "o" and "u".

Acknowledgements

The Publisher would like to thank the following copyright holders:

With thanks to Mary Evans Picture Library for permission to use the images on pages 7, 9 and 10

With thanks to iStockphoto.com for permission to use the image on page 8

With thanks to Rex Features for permission to use the images on pages 11, 13, 14, 15, 16, 17, 19, 20 and 21

With thanks to Alamy for permission to use the images on pages 12 and 18

'Desert Places' by Robert Frost from *Selected Poems* 2011, published by Oxford University Press. Reprinted by permission of the Random House Group

'Dulce et Decorum Est', 'The Dead-Beat' and 'The Send-Off' from *Wilfred Owen: The War Poems*, edited by Jon Stallworthy (Chatto and Windus, 1994)

'On Being a Woman' and 'Condolence' by Dorothy Parker from *The Collected Dorothy Parker*

'Dover' © 1937 and 'The More Loving One' © 1957 by W.H. Auden and Louis MacNeice, renewed. Reprinted by permission of Curtis Brown, Ltd

'Equality' and 'Kin' by Maya Angelou from *The Complete Collected Poems* by Maya Angelou published by Virago Press. Reprinted by permission of Little, Brown Book Group Ltd

'Still', 'Jumper' & 'Long Distance II' published with permission from Tony Harrison © Tony Harrison

'Faint Praise', 'The Sitter' and 'Flowers' reprinted by permission of United Agents on behalf of: Wendy Cope

'It is Time to Tidy Up Your Life' and 'Armada' copyright © Brian Patten 2007. Reproduced by permission of the author c/o Rogers, Coleridge & White Ltd., 20 Powis Mews, London, W11 1JN

'The Goose and the Gander' and 'Volumes' by Jo Shapcott from *Her Book, Poems 1988-98*

'Anyone Can Draw a Line' by Sophie Hannah with permission of the author

'Valentine' and 'History' copyright © Owen Sheers 2005. Reproduced by permission of the author c/o Rogers, Coleridge & White Ltd., 20 Powis Mews, London W11 1JN

'Against Road-building' from *Leaving and Leaving You* by Sophie Hannah (Carcanet Press Limited, 1999)

'The Road Not Taken' by Robert Frost from *The Complete Poems of Robert Frost*. Reprinted by permission of the Random House Group

'Don't Say I Said' from *Pessimism for Beginners* by Sophie Hannah (Carcanet Press Limited, 2007)